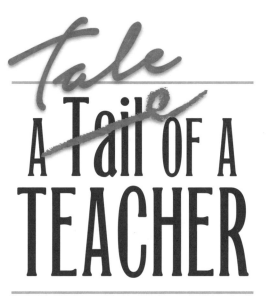

A ~~Tail~~ _Tale_ OF A TEACHER

Roger Stoufer

For more information, contact:
Minnesota Heritage Publishing
205 Ledlie Lane, Suite 125
Mankato, MN 56001
www.mnheritage.com

ISBN: 978-0-9850937-7-8

Library of Congress Catalog Number: 2014948733

Published by Minnesota Heritage Publishing

Printed in the United States of America
by Corporate Graphics, North Mankato, MN

First Edition

Edited by Betsy Sherman

Cover Design and Layout by Michael Sellner

Dedication

This book is dedicated to my wife, Beverly. Without her prodding and encouragement it likely would not have been written, and definitely not published.

A special thank you to Julie Schrader: Minnesota Heritage Publishing and Betsy Sherman for their expertise in editing and publishing.

Preface

Everyone attends them, but only a few people really know what happens, in schools, and, because of them. People; also; seldom consider how what happens outside school affects what happens inside.

Schools are the milieu for students and teachers who work in them. The school's primary purpose is educating students to function effectively in society. That, however, is mixed with its role in teaching students to navigate relationships, to assume leadership and subordinate roles among peers, and to develop necessary coping skills needed to solve problems. These challenges that confront administrators, teachers, and students hourly in an overcrowded, restricted environment are demanding. All three of these groups are composed of strong-minded people with varying social and cultural backgrounds. Despite these difficulties and differences, and contrary to much of what is heard in public discourse, most schools function admirably in meeting their responsibilities.

In American public schools, each student's experience is unique. I began by failing first grade in a small rural school and completed with a master's degree and 60 additional graduate credits from a university with 15,000 students—none of which was planned. My story, unlike some, has less to do with the credits earned and more to do with my life experiences in acquiring them—experiences that are integrally related to my teaching and learning.

While this story includes an account of my own educational experience as a student, and tales of outstanding teachers and administrators who were my colleagues, relationships with memorable students who carved a niche into my soul, and the impact of my personal life experiences on my career, it is primarily focused on my training to become a good teacher. In 1965 the school board chair in Stewart, Minnesota told us negotiators that, "Stewart is a teacher training school, and I believe you are now trained."

I knew he was telling me to move on to a bigger district if I wanted a higher salary, but I also knew I wasn't fully trained. I had a lot to learn before I could consider myself a skilled teacher. Some of my training so far was the result of working with excellent teachers who had mentored me, some had happened through magnetic students who motivated me to teach better, and some was the result of my willingness to risk failure. Later, though, much was the result of a national recognition of the necessity to improve instruction, driven by substandard scores on standardized tests. A wide variety of solutions were proposed. Some failed, and some provided growth but none solved the problems that confronted us. My examination and interpretation of all of these efforts is shared herein.

Our schools are filled with outstanding teachers. Many of whom stay up late correcting papers and planning almost every evening. Most attend extra-curricular events to support their student's development outside of class. This account of teaching experiences includes stories of educators who go above and beyond. They motivate their colleagues and inspire their students. These individuals are the models for the rest.

The memorable students whose stories told here are not just the great scholars. Rather, they are those who touched my heart and by accident or fate became a significant part of my life.

The need to fix the flaws in our education system continues to dominate many news stories. Politicians and lawmakers seem to want to "throw out the baby with the bath water." Part of this is likely motivated by an effort to destroy public employee unions. Some pundits, politicians and satirists paint teachers as greedy, lazy, uninformed, self-serving bureaucrats.

Unions too should rethink their role. While serving to promote and protect teachers, they must work with school districts in the effort to change the learning culture. They must send the message that schools require students to put forth their best effort while in class. They can also help teachers improve their image. The Mallard Fillmore comic strip which depicts teachers as lazy, uninformed and greedy is winning the image battle. While most communities may view their own teachers as skilled professionals, the stereotypical portrait prevails nationally.

To combat this, many schools are joining together to develop a professional learning community in which teachers and administrators meet regularly to share their ideas for what works in the classroom. In developing a list of best practices they are integrating some of the earlier efforts to improve the system like mentoring programs and outcome based education. This demands satisfactory results on core curricular concepts. These communities meet regularly and share successes and failures. In so doing they are continuing to develop a sound list of best practices in the classroom. As Cindy Amoroso, the curriculum director in Mankato, Minnesota says, "Teachers need to be laser focused on what they want students to learn." They also need to keep the public informed of their laser focused efforts.

To that, I would also add: "They must do that without sucking the joy and humanity out of the classroom." I am convinced that is possible if educational researchers, government leaders at all levels, teacher training institutions, unions and schools—both public and private—work together.

Instead of only criticizing each other these entities must heighten awareness of the importance of learning and share their successes with each other. The result we all seek is a more informed citizenry that can solve its problems with greater skill and confidence.

Table of Contents

CHALKBOARD ERA

Echo, MN Grades 1-12 1945-1958

A Most Inauspicious Beginning

Attending school
was not to be,
at home with mom
was best for me.

All of us have what is known as a Johari window. A peek into this window gives a view of the total of all our life experiences from the time we were born until the present. A second window, however, overlaps a major portion of the first, limiting the content of what others see. What they see is only that part of our experiences that we are willing to share. This second window differs in size and shape for each of our acquaintances. We share ourselves through this overlapping window based on our level of confidence and the amount of trust we have built with our acquaintances.

1

Most of us have a few deep, dark secrets. We keep them from our spouses, our closest friends, and often even our counselors. The state of our mental health is reflected largely by how much of ourselves we share with others. Deeply held secrets may damage our psyche. To defuse the power of these secrets and mitigate the pain they cause, we share them with people we trust.

Something I rarely reveal is that I failed first grade, which, because there was no kindergarten, was my first school experience. While I'm unsure what exactly led to my failure, the memories I have lead me to believe it was a combination of health issues and immaturity.

There were, of course, other factors among them. These included poverty, lack of preparation, low expectations from the school and my family, and a substandard educational system. But the main cause of my failure was me.

Children born into poverty are far less likely to succeed in school. When I was born, my father worked for the Works Progress Administration. We shared a house in Echo, Minn. with another family. A cardboard wall divided the living room and two bedrooms, and the kitchen and outhouse were both shared. Arguments sometimes erupted between Dad and Mr. Hagedorn, his tenant partner. Not long after they had a fistfight, we moved.

In 1944 Dad took a job as a farm laborer with a wealthy, local farmer named, Tom Homme, and we moved into a home near the Homme farm, about a quarter of a mile from my mother's parents, Grandma and Grandpa Lecy. We still had an outhouse and our drinking water now came from a neighbor's well. Water for Saturday night baths was heated on our wood burning kitchen range. The rent was $10.00 dollars per month but dad's salary was only $75.00. When dad quit the farm job to work in the local granite quarry, he earned a dollar an hour. Working forty hour weeks, he earned one-hundred-seventy dollars per month. We were still among the poorest people in the area.

Mom and Dad had little time or ability to prepare me or my siblings—older Brother Larry and Sister Faye—for school. Mom cooked, sewed, cleaned, canned, did laundry, and looked after the children while Dad went to work at the quarry, repaired local telephone lines, raised and butchered livestock, repaired the car and kept the table stocked with fish and wild game. Our souls were considered more valuable than our intellects. There was no newspaper, no books other than the Bible in the house, and paper, pencil and crayons were scarce. We started school with no practice in reading, writing or ciphering. Our intellects were a blank slate.

In some ways our parent's low expectations of us may have made things easier. Neither had graduated from high school. Mom stayed home with her parents and dad worked for local farmers. In that respect their expectations of us emulated their parent's educational goals for them.

My Uncle, Buddy, who worked on our grandparent's farm next to us, often said, "That high school education stuff is a bunch of crap. If you worked and saved your money those four years, you could save a couple thousand dollars. That'd be enough to buy a tractor and get you started farming."

The community did little to compensate for family shortcomings. The school district was responsible mainly for enrolling students and providing transportation for rural children. There was no kindergarten or preschool program. Assessments of new students were unheard of and teachers did not meet with families to help support them in school.

As if that weren't enough, my first grade teacher was neither very nurturing nor appealing. Her dark hair stood high above her forehead and was pulled back with something that looked like twine. She never smiled and spoke in guttural tones. Looking at her and listening to her made me anxious.

The demands she made of me were impossible. She wanted me to sit still and listen, when all I wanted to do was move around and talk. I thought surely there is room for compromise. *Half the time I'll sit still and listen, and the other half I'll move around and talk. That seems fair.*

Apparently it didn't seem fair to her. Every time I moved or talked, she sent me to the cloakroom where a chair sat facing the plastered wall. In a few weeks I knew where every pimple was on that wall.

As I pondered the problems I was having in school, I concluded my Uncle Buddy's theory about not needing high school was wrong. It didn't go far enough. Not only was high school unnecessary but so was first grade. I decided to quit school.

Since the law wouldn't allow this, I followed the pattern set by most petty criminals and circumvented the law. Every Sunday evening, I either felt or faked some malaise and used it to my advantage with my mother. Mom was easy because I was her baby. It was likely that the death of my cousin, Lavonne Arndt, from leukemia a few years earlier helped me in my efforts to fool mom.

After several missed school days my parents made an appointment with the family doctor. Dr. Peterson, an older white haired gentleman, was affectionately called dollar Pete because that was his charge for an office call. When Dad asked, "What do I owe you, Doc?" Dr. Peterson responded, "Oh, I guess that'll be about a dollar."

On our first visit Dollar Pete pricked my ear for a blood sample, put it under his microscope, and said, "I don't think it's leukemia. His blood looks pretty good." After that, mom was more gullible than ever.

By the end of the year I had missed over 40 days of school. My teacher sent a note to mom informing her, "It might be best for Roger if he repeats first grade. He missed too much school to gain all of the skills necessary to be successful in second grade." Because she taught a combination of first and second grade, she knew what was needed to advance.

Like our parents, my older siblings dropped out of school before graduating. My younger sister Susan and I both earned college degrees—thanks to several dynamics in our family, school, and community that eventually changed.

To prevent dropouts a contractual partnership must be reached between family, school and community that addresses the issues which prevent students like my siblings from succeeding in our schools. The importance of an educated, truth-seeking, literate, problem solving population is too critical to the success of our democracy, and to the individuals who are left by the wayside to fail in this endeavor.

Primary School

In first grade my school day began on a bus. Because we lived at the end of the route, we were the last to be picked up. We could sleep later in the mornings, but the ride home seemed endless, especially that day when my pants were torn off.

I was sitting safely by Larry, who was then in fifth grade, when Marvin Olson, a high school student, urged me to come sit by him. I fell for the pitch.

"Come sit by me little Stoufer. It's a rule on this bus that all first-grade boys are initiated. It's really fun. You're gonna love it!"

Larry whispered, "Don't go. Those older guys are mean."

But I was curious and thought, *What harm can come to me on a school bus?* Later I added the word "naïve" to my vocabulary.

Before I could sit down Olson grabbed me and held up me in the air, while Sandquist unbuttoned my trousers; and pulled them off. It took me a second to realize I was in the aisle of the bus wearing only underwear. Everyone on the bus; except the driver, Henry Iverson, was focused on me and all of them were laughing. Henry stared straight ahead at the narrow gravel road.

Captain Marvel said, "Shazam" when he needed strength. Sir

Gawaine Le Cour Hardy said, "Rumplesnitz" when he needed extra power to kill dragons. Without a magic word I had no chance to destroy these evil creatures holding my slacks.

I played my only trump card. "If you don't give my pants back, my brother Larry will beat you up!"

Sandquist responded by moving forward, and grabbing Larry who in a nanosecond was standing beside me wearing only his underwear with the others hooting at him.

Probably five miles down the road Olson laughingly handed me my slacks saying, "Gopher nuts! Better put your pants back on" he said, "You look silly sitting there in your underwear."

Henry finally stopped the bus letting Phillip Ratchie, a high school senior, exit. I prayed that he would storm back and rescue me from my two tormentors and throw them off the bus. Alas he didn't. I was later to know Henry as a nurturing grandfather figure on the bus, but he had failed me here. The only solace was the Stoufer boys made history by their dual depantsing.

That whole episode taught me to be more careful about whom to sit near on the bus. There were no boys my age but I enjoyed visiting with Verla Mae Hetle and Patty Walseth who were about my age.

Middle Elementary

My third grade teacher, Mrs. Pashke, ironically thought my first grade retention was unnecessary. Since she taught a combination third and fourth grade, she tried to "catch me up" by having me complete all the assignments for both third and fourth grades in one year. She hoped to advance me straight from third to fifth grade. But at the end of the school year she wrote on the back of my report card, "I will be unable to advance Roger to fifth grade next year. The Department of Education frowns on students skipping grades." So I repeated first and fourth grade.

While in third grade Dollar Pete's son, Kenneth, a surgeon in Marshall, Minnesota determined I suffered from an infected appendix. Since we had neither money nor health insurance, he offered an affordable payment system. Because he was a childhood friend of dad's, he also reduced his fee. Dad cried when he made him the offer. After the surgery my energy and school performance both improved.

Fifth grade, though, started almost as badly as first. Hib Hackbarth, the new Peace Lutheran preacher's kid, had a smart mouth. He was new to our school and to Minnesota and he didn't seem to like either one. I made the mistake of asking him, "Where you from?"

If he would have simply said, "Michigan" that would have been fine but he added, "We're going to kick your Gopher's butts on Saturday."

That taunt was too much. I replied "I hear those Wolverines are so scared that they're considering not showing up."

He clenched his fists and retorted, "We'll see who's scared. Put'em up or shut up!"

We were in the boys' bathroom, and I didn't really want to fight but my honor was at stake. Hoping to delay I said, "If we do fight they'll be finding pieces of you back in Michigan when it's over."

He shouted back, "There won't be anything left of you to find."

My classmate, Gordie Oie, who had been enjoying the melee warned, "Knock it off! Hegdahl's coming!"

Actually, she wasn't coming; she was present. She grabbed me by my collar and Hackbarth by his and towed us to the classroom. Upon arrival she positioned us on opposite sides of her desk and instructed, "Don't move an inch, and don't say a word until I say to." Her tone left no room for disagreement.

When the class returned from recess Mrs. Hegdahl settled everyone down and announced, "Roger and Hilbert behaved in an inappropriate manner in the boy's room. They were rude to each other and the other boys present. They are now going to apologize to the class and follow that by apologizing to each other, shaking hands, and promising this will never happen again."

Neither of us protested. We stumbled quickly through our apologies and promises and returned to our desks. My anger had dissipated and was replaced by a flood of relief and embarrassment. I liked Mrs. Hegdahl and didn't want to upset her.

The Hegdahls had moved to Echo from Frost, Minn., where Pearly Hegdahl had been the school superintendent. His parents had retired from farming near Belview and he was leaving his career in education to operate the family farm. While waiting for his parents to move from the homestead, the family of five lived in a small apartment above the hardware store on Main Street in Echo. Although Mrs. Hegdahl was my teacher, she was not the most important family member to me.

Kathy, the youngest, was in my class and she was cute. She had short blond hair, cut flat at the base of her neck, with bangs across her forehead. Her cheekbones were high and she had blue eyes that danced when she talked. Her legs were as thin as the legs on our kitchen chairs. We had only four girls in our class, so any new ones were welcome, but she was more than welcome.

I knew Mrs. Hegdahl respected me. She often asked me to read out loud to the class and told me "Roger, you are an excellent reader." I tried to read aloud with more "feeling" every time she asked me even though my classmate, Ronnie Nyberg, gave me dirty looks whenever she praised me.

Mrs. Hegdahl made math into a competitive sport. Almost daily we had speed drills in addition, subtraction, multiplication, and division. Even though Patty Walseth and some others were smarter than me, I sped through the problems, rapidly scribbling my numbers onto the paper, often winning the math races. Mrs. Hegdahl always smiled as she announced the winner.

Our regular math assignments weren't as much fun as the speed drills. I sometimes didn't pay enough attention to detail when completing them. Once Mrs. Hegdahl held my paper for a second before she gave it to me and said sadly, "Pearly helps me correct math papers in the evening. I always give him your paper because he likes to correct the *good papers*. He was disappointed last night."

As she handed me the paper I saw–12 circled in red. After that I made sure not to disappoint Pearly again.

Eventually the Hegdahls moved to the farmhouse house near Belview and took their beautiful daughter with them. Mrs. Hegdahl left me with a new confidence in my abilities that may never have arisen otherwise.

Junior High

When I was in junior high school our family moved from the country into the village of Echo. Dad took a position with The Echo Granite Works that paid better. Our rental home had indoor plumbing, gas heat and a telephone bringing us from the 19th century into the 20th. The improved circumstances also seemed to mellow my father's temper, which helped the whole family.

Our "new" rental home was less than a block from the school. I made friends with kids my age, and we gathered together at its playground. The school became a place of joy all the year around. Band, chorus, sports, class plays, FFA and almost every other extracurricular activity offered were an important part of my life. Teachers encouraged us to be deeply involved in the school.

I was a part of something special—The class of 1958.

I also became part of the community. That meant my free time was spent at the *Hurry Back Inn* and the Pool Hall. There, at the age of 14, I socialized with everyone, from the town drunk to the mayor.

Seventh and eighth graders were placed in a class taught by Hildred Riley. The teaching model, which was the same as the elementary grades, was driven by a small enrollment and an even smaller budget, not by the desire to provide the best learning environment for adolescent students.

Miss Riley taught in the district for over 30 years. She was striking in her appearance with dark eyes, very dark black hair, and sharp angular facial features. She was only average in stature but something about her commanded attention. She was a devout Catholic in our deeply Lutheran community. Old timers said she had trained to be a nun and teach in a parochial school, but that circumstances led her back to care for her parents on their farm near Echo, where she accepted a teaching position and lived at home. When her parents died, she continued to live with her brother, Bob. She never married and dedicated her life to teaching in our school, just as she likely would have done as a nun teaching in a parochial school.

The whole community recognized Miss Riley as a masterful teacher. Administrators and school board members probably deliberately placed her among adolescents so that her strong sense of discipline and solid organizational skills could be a match for their impulsive hormone-driven behavior. The leaders of the school system placed their trust in her, and usually that resulted in a successful learning environment.

Besides the unpredictable behavior of junior high students, Miss Riley also faced the problem of increasing class size as rural students from country elementary schools came into town to complete their public schooling. Her class enrollment added three or four new students to the number of students taught in sixth grade. When this additional class size was coupled with challenging students, even she had problems. That was the case my seventh grade year.

She normally managed the difficulties of classroom management with ease. While preparing seventh graders for a lesson, she had eighth graders working on the new material she had just presented to them. One change in the junior high curriculum that caused a problem was the replacement of recess with physical education. Boys and girls were separated in PE classes. Since Miss Riley was the PE teacher, as well as the classroom teacher, she was forced to leave, unsupervised in the classroom, the group not participating in physical education while she taught the other. That meant trouble.

Several of the eighth-grade boys including "Snoose" Peterson," "Lover Boy Lulum" and "Herby Hitter" were filled with mischief and saw this as an opportunity to carry it out. They left notes saying, "R U Horny" in girl's textbooks. Desks were moved around so taller girls would return from PE to find that their knees touched the bottom of the desks. A condom was placed in a mature appearing girl's textbook. Once, two students, Sharon Less and Phyllis Hart, said they didn't feel well and were left in the classroom, while Miss Riley left to teach PE to the other girls. One of the boys, probably "Snoose," who openly carried Copenhagen in his shirt pocket, walked by their desks to sharpen his pencil and helped himself to a "feel" from each of them.

This resulted in corrective measures by Miss Riley. Girls were never again left without supervision in the classroom. Our classroom was located just outside the gym floor, so girl's physical education classes were held in the gym and the classroom door was always open. She did her best to supervise both areas.

Miss Riley was a master teacher who had been given an impossible task. Asking her to manage the situation was like telling a custodian to clean the floor with engine oil. All the ingredients for failure were in the recipe which had been written by the administration and school board to save money. Even the best teachers need the proper tools to build a quality classroom.

The next year the seventh and eighth grades were separated and Miss Riley was again my teacher, as she was assigned the eighth grade. However, big changes had been made. The eighth graders were in a smaller classroom on the second floor. Miss Riley was able to spend more time helping us when we had trouble with an assignment. My grades improved, and I was chosen to represent the school in the county spelling contest.

Miss Riley gave me a list of words to study to prepare. The contest consisted of a written test and an oral bee. Based on the results of the written test, the top 10 spellers qualified for the spelldown. During the spelldown, when a student misspelled a word, they were out of the competition and had to sit down. I was overjoyed when the moderator of the event announced the top ten qualifiers, my name was among them.

I did fine with my first word in the bee, "thoroughbred" but had to return to my seat after spelling *"truesew."*

Neighboring villages in Minnesota often create arch rivalries that include all aspects of community and school life. Belview, five miles east of Echo, was our adversary. We matched up fairly evenly in high school sports but the Echo school band was so bad it was nearly non-existent. Belview parents proudly attended concerts where their children flawlessly performed overtures and Sousa marches while the Echo parents, who could afford to pay for piano lessons, listened to their children struggle through *"Twinkle, Twinkle Little Star"* in their living rooms.

To build their successful music program the Norwegian Lutheran residents of Belview had broken with tradition and hired a Polish band director named Fiokowski. He was an accomplished musician, fundraiser, recruiter and organizer. Under his leadership, every high school student in Belview owned a musical instrument and most could play them.

Fiokowsi had solicited funds from local merchants and farmers and outfitted his band with the most expensive and attractive band uniforms in the state. Soliciting money for band uniforms from Norwegian farmers was a Herculean task but he had accomplished it. The band was impressive even when it tuned up the instruments.

For Echo to match the Belview program it needed to find a low budget music salesman like the famed Harold Hill who sold band instruments to the conservative parents in River City, Iowa. The Echo German community would have preferred a Herman Schmidt while the Echo Norsks wanted a Henry Pederson but the messiah who built the band came to Echo when I was in seventh grade. He was a youthful Dane named Bud Christiansen.

His first step was requiring all students, one grade level at a time, to take a music listening test. When they passed with remarkably high scores, he asked them to choose their preferred band instrument, write it on a form and give it to him. Not knowing any instruments by name I followed the lead of Patty Walseth, who sat in front of me, and *we* chose to play a clarinet.

Mr. Christiansen then met with the students and their parents—either in their homes or at school. At those sessions he and a representative from the Redwood Falls music store had all the band instruments present. Students were allowed to pick them up, blow into them, beat on them or do whatever was required to make noise. In no time at all he had sold instruments and lesson books to most of the parents. To accomplish purchasing uniforms he mirrored Belview' model with similar success.

When his students had their instruments and lesson books, he scheduled lessons which were rigorous beyond anything they had ever experienced. Soon; the band was playing at sporting events where the noise was loud enough to cover some of the squeaks from the budding clarinetists and off beat umpahs from the tuba. In the spring of his first year The Echo High School Band performed a concert that included *the Traveler Overture* by Forrest Buchtel and *Stars and Stripes Forever* by John Philip Sousa. **Eat your heart out Belview.** Our Dane, Christianson, had equaled your Polish Fiokowski.

Although my parents couldn't afford a new clarinet for me, Mr. Christiansen found a used one and arranged a payment schedule. I never became an accomplished clarinetist but I recognized the miracle and was part of it. I attended band rehearsal every day playing clarinet with Patty Walseth, John Salls, and the Eskeldson girls. My cousin and classmate; Joy Arndt; played baritone, my friends Hib Hackbarth and Dennis Johnson played trombone and my second cousin, Myron Lecy, frequently solocd while he played first chair trumpet.

High School

When Mr.Christiansen, accepted a position as band director in Hector, Minn, he was replaced by a Mr. Busch. I suspect Mr Busch was a skilled musician but he lacked Mr. Christiansen's zest for life. Some of the seniors in band decided to drive him out of town. Margie Crane was the most active of the pack. She played bass drum and would mess up the beat, playing either too softly or too loudly, and plotted with other musicians to create disturbances. When Mr. Busch corrected them, they argued with him trying to make him angry. They were relentless and merciless. Band practice was worse than ninth grade algebra.

Other doors began to open in ninth grade. Ninth grade boys had the chance to compete against other teams in football. Before we could practice we had to pass a physical, which I failed. I had a hernia that required surgery. Football would have to wait for a year.

I had looked forward to what high school had in store for me for a long time. Celebrating homecoming was one of the exciting new events I most anticipated. That, however, did not go smoothly.

Long standing tradition in Echo held that ninth grade students built the homecoming coronation bonfire. Shirley Meier had decreed that our class would build the best bonfire in history. For days we had gathered brush and piled it for pick up. After school one day Shirley's dad helped us haul it to the burn site near the school, where after the snake dance the next night, the fire was to be lit. The homecoming pep fest and Queen's Coronation were to be held in the shadows of the flames.

That night I was just about to doze off, when I heard a noise that sounded like stones hitting the side of the house beside my second-floor window. My classmate, Shirley Meier and her friend, Diane Grane, were standing below calling softly, "Roger, Roger!"

I opened the window. Tearfully and both speaking at once they said, "Our bonfire's burning! Somebody lit our bonfire!

I threw on my clothes and hurried downstairs. As I passed my parents room, dad sleepily called out, "What's going on?"

"Nothing serious," I said. Shirley Meier's outside. "I guess someone burned our bonfire."

"Don't you go anywhere," he ordered.

I could smell the smoke from the fire when I opened the door. Shirley and Diane rushed toward me "Those Belview kids are trying to ruin our homecoming. They lit our woodpile just to be mean. Do you think our teachers will let us out of class tomorrow to gather more brush?"

"Let's go watch the fire burn," I said. "At least we'll get that much out of it."

We had gathered the most brush ever and were—"busting our buttons"—with pride as we looked forward to the upcoming events. Now it was all going up in smoke, literally. As we walked we watched the flames shoot skyward. Bo Hustad, our town cop, was already there when we arrived. He offered little consolation.

"No! I can't arrest the Belview kids for this mischief," he said. "It's not that serious and we can't prove they did it." The girls' continued pleas were to no avail.

The next night after the snake dance wove through the downtown business district, and the coronation ceremonies for the new queen were held in the gymnasium.

I had big plans for homecoming night. I was anxious but determined to seek dad's approval to park the family car on the field's sidelines at the homecoming game. Everyone who arrived early enough could sit in their cars to watch the game, and I would really be a big shot if my pals sat in *my car* with **me** behind the wheel.

It was a pleasant surprise when dad responded to my request. "I don't see why not. Here's the deal though. Drive the car up now and leave it there and don't bring it home until the game's ended and everyone else has left."

"Wow! How could life be any better?" I foolishly thought.

I don't recall the score of the game or any of the plays or players. I do, however, recall what happened afterward with a remarkable clarity considering that almost 60 years have passed since then. At the end of the game my car was loaded with spectators, most of whom pleaded for a ride downtown. Violet Luepke, the girl who that night had made my heart skip a beat, took it a step further when she implored, "Please, Roger, let me drive. I know how."

Seeking a "closer" relationship, I wasted no time but suggested, "Let's go out by Speed Corner. That'll kill some time allowing the traffic going downtown to empty out of here."

Vi sat behind the steering wheel, shifted into low gear, pressed the starter button on the 48 Plymouth, disengaged the clutch and lurched forward a few feet. The engine stalled. She repeated the process several times before swerving toward one of the wooden poles holding the field lights. Although I was growing apprehensive about her driving skills, I feared offending her might quell any thoughts of possible fondness that she might be indulging. I kept my mouth shut and prayed.

Finally, we lurched forward without stalling the engine and headed toward the exit. The car filled with a roar as Gene, Shirley and Diane rejoiced with their loud halleluiahs. We shot out the exit and made a left onto Main Street where Vi shifted into second gear nearly throwing us into the windshield as she dropped the clutch, causing the car to decelerate abruptly. Then she accelerated even more abruptly. This happened three or four times. Each time, I rocked back and forth so hard that my head slammed first into the dash then the seat. "Oh my God," I thought. "What next?"

I was soon to find out. Speed Corner, a T in the road a half mile out of town, was famed as the starting point for drag races. As we approached it, Vi speeded up. Swinging wildly into a U-turn, she headed directly toward the steep embankment across the road. The car veered down the embankment, tilting onto two wheels before Vi braked violently leaving the car hanging precariously on the side of the embankment.

After exiting from the car to a secure position on the road, we looked at its position in the ditch, and tried to determine the best alternatives for getting it safely back into my dad's garage. The decision was quickly made not to risk driving the car out. The best choices seemed either to "run away" or to locate help. A farmer named Charlie who was known more for his overindulgence of alcohol than for his agrarian skills, lived a few rods away. Gene suggested, "If Charlie pulls you out with his tractor, your dad will never need to know."

Like Huck Finn's plan to escape an abusive father by feigning his own death, the idea seemed foolproof. We created a story to tell Charlie and chose Gene to be the storyteller

We knocked on Charlie's front door repeatedly and after a long wait he appeared. His appearance was disheveled and his speech slurred. He examined us carefully. "Why in Hell did you get me out of bed?"

He paused and I thought, "This is not going well."

Gene jumped in quickly, starting the story smoothly, "Charlie, we were making a U-turn out here when our headlights failed. It was so dark we couldn't see the road, so we missed the turn and got stuck in the ditch. Could you tow us out?"

"You guys been drinking?" Charlie responded gruffly.

"No sir!" I blurted.

"Any girls with you?"

I had found my voice and spoke with more bravado, "No Sir."

We had anticipated this question and had told the girls to hide in Charlie's grove until we gave them the all clear.

"Damn it, I don't like this! Follow me!" Charlie led us to his old H Farmall tractor, started it, and ordered, "Jump on the bar and hold on tight to the back of the seat." Dropping the clutch he lifted the front end of the tractor off the ground.

"Vi drives better than this guy," I thought.

When Charlie pulled the tractor next to the car, he exploded with a string of curse words concluding with "Jesus Christ! You guys damn near rolled this thing over. You were damn lucky." He backed up to the front bumper, and attached a chain to his hitch and my bumper. Looking at Gene he said, "Get your ass in that car and steer it out of the ditch as I pull."

We had prepared to pay Charlie an appropriate fee for his services, by pooling all of our meager resources. When he unhitched the chain I handed him the $1.57 and said, "Thanks."

"What the hell is this?" he muttered. I could hear the girls laughing in his nearby grove. I was euphoric when Charlie climbed on his tractor and left us without another word.

"I dodged a bullet tonight," I thought to myself. Then I glanced at the bumper and saw the bent front bumper guard that Charlie had attached his chain to. There would be no easy way out of this.

Mom and Dad were still at Bernice and Herman's, when I got home. I parked the car in the garage, inching it tightly against the front wall, and quickly went to bed.

When the sun rose I hadn't slept yet. Dad and I were to set monuments in the Wood Lake cemetery all day. I hoped he'd already noticed the damage to the car. I knew he'd kill me when I told him, and I wanted to get it over. He brought me out of my deep thoughts shouting, "Come on, Rog! We've got work to do. If we don't get moving, we'll be there until dark."

I said little all day as we worked together mixing concrete, digging holes, and placing tombstones in proper alignment in the cemetery. Dad, who rarely noticed my behavior, said, "You're pretty quiet today, Tony. Did you chase girls too much last night?"

I didn't respond, until after we'd accomplished our day's work. Then I told him about the accident and was relieved at his measured response. I was careful not to tell him Violet was driving. That remained a secret for another in thirty years.

By that time I had purchased a summer home on Lake Geneva in Alexandria, Minnesota and Mom and Dad were visiting my wife, Bev and I and our kids. Dad left the cabin to fish by himself early in the morning. Somehow, while in thirty feet of water, he dropped my five horse Johnson trolling motor into the lake.

As he was explaining the "accident" to me and apologizing, I interrupted him and said, "Save you're apology. Remember when I bent the bumper guard on your 48 Plymouth? Let me tell you the whole story. I think you'll agree we're about even."

Probably the most significant part of my ninth grade year is what I didn't learn. Our algebra teacher, Mr. Rakke, in his first year teaching, lacked classroom management skills. Sadly, he received no assistance from the administration. His class was noisy and chaotic. Even though he knew his material and presented it well, little learning took place in his classroom. To learn algebra, students had to take their books home and review what had been presented through the chaotic din. I didn't do that. My basic math skills were strong, but algebra was sequential and once I fell behind, I was lost in the woods of solving for X. I couldn't find a path through those woods without a strong guide. This caused trouble for me during my college years.

Algebra, biology, physics and chemistry were core subjects required in college. To meet graduation requirements, students must satisfactorily complete three of them. All required the ability to solve for X. I lacked it. In college I avoided algebra and muddled my way through physics and chemistry earning C's. I realized that although students might be able to create a chaotic environment in the classroom, it must not be allowed to happen. Administrators and teachers are responsible for preventing it.

Unlike Mr. Rakke's classroom, ninth grade social studies was an academic Garden of Eden. Mr. Avery was pleasant and relaxed, but controlled. His presentations were skilled. He involved us in thoughtful discussions and monitored our study time, keeping us on task. We knew we were expected to "learn" in his class and respected his ability to help us.

Other classes were routine. Mrs. Hvam, our English teacher, was a sweet, older woman who required us to read and complete book reports. They followed an organized form that was vital to clear writing. Mr. Schoen, our head football coach and principal also taught ninth-grade science. He was out of the classroom much of the time tending to principal duties. He listened to the class on the public address system. We could hear it click off and on. Sometimes when it clicked on, he would proclaim loudly, "Kissner and Stoufer, shut-up and get to work." The work consisted mainly of answering the questions at the back of each chapter in the book and handing them in. We never saw them again. I also was required to take a course in agriculture from Mr. Knudson. We learned how to rotate crops, test milk for butterfat and develop a balanced diet for pigs. I haven't used those skills much since.

The curriculum in Echo was largely stagnant. The world was rapidly changing and our lessons weren't. I enjoyed school and was provided the basics and a wonderful adolescent experience. But, with a larger budget and stronger, more insightful leadership, school might have done even more to prepare me for the future.

Tenth Grade

I loved basketball. As a rural elementary school student from a family with limited resources, I had been denied the opportunity to attend most school events. A few times though, Dad took me to varsity basketball games.

The gymnasium where they were held was in the center of the elementary school. The classrooms were behind the two rows of spectator chairs abutting the black out-of-bounds line for the gymnasium. Fans cheered the team and booed the officials from the two-tiered balcony above these chairs. A basket hung on the wall at the South end of the gym while the other was hung by metal pipes connected to floor of the stage, where the band performed during games. There was little room to maneuver under either basket. Although the gym was a crackerbox, for a while it was the Williams Arena of my little universe.

At the beginning of the tenth grade year I had high hopes of securing a starting position on the B squad and earning limited playing time on the varsity. My shooting skills were above average but my self-evaluation failed to include a lack of height, a small frame and average speed. These were quickly noticed by coach Schoen.

During practice he would see an opening and yell, "Drive for the basket, Stoufer. They're giving you two points." Or when I was beaten on defense, I would hear, "Stay in front of your man. Don't give him that easy shot." Despite those easily noticeable mistakes, I was unaware that my future in basketball was limited. I persevered.

Once, during a game with Wood Lake, I was sitting on the bench as our B team was being slaughtered. The coach suddenly blurted "Stoufer, Get in there and shoot. Nobody else can make a basket. Let's see if you can."

When Wood Lake scored, the buzzer sounded and the official waved me into the game. Finally, I was getting a chance to show my stuff. I inbounded the ball to Doug Parsons who dribbled it up the court and passed it back to me. Seeing an opening, I made my move with reckless abandon. The problem was that I dribbled into the corner, where I was trapped by two of Wood Lake's better defenders. In desperation I used the only weapon left in my arsenal—I pivoted and tossed up an awkward hook shot which, by an act of God, floated perfectly into the basket without touching the rim. Coach Schoen wasn't impressed.

The buzzer sounded again following my basket and Myron Lecy came onto the floor. He pointed to me. I was already being replaced. My head dropped as I walked to the bench where Coach Schoen met me saying. "What in God's name were you doing? You take the ball to the basket not to the corner. Sit down."

I didn't play much after that. Usually I replaced someone in foul trouble or played after the outcome of the game had been decided. Like Rudy, in the movie "Hoosier," I continued to be a non-contributing member of the team. While this did not fulfill my boyhood dreams, I did learn not to be a quitter, to accept my role whatever it was, and to learn whatever I could from each role I played.

Later, during my years as an educator I enjoyed serving as an assistant basketball coach and utilizing the nuances I had learned in the hundreds of games I attended and watched. I truly enjoyed the "Rudy" role in basketball throughout my teaching career. Not bad for a kid who dribbled into the corner of the gym instead of going for the basket.

Surprisingly, biology was my favorite class in 10th grade. Mr. MrKonich, our teacher, was also the assistant football coach. He had clear expectations. He often said, "Do your best in everything you do and if that's not good enough do better."

In football practice he never wore pads but always kept an older black and red leather helmet nearby. If anyone made a bad block or tackle, he called us aside, put on the helmet, and demonstrated the correct technique. Then he lined up in the backfield and declared, "Unless you use what I just taught you on me, I'm going to push you out of the way like you were a bag of feathers." He'd slap on that helmet and roar, "Give me your best shot. You know I'm coming at you."

That was also the way he taught Biology. He warned, "I'm giving you the toughest test you've ever taken and here's what you need to know to pass it." My natural inclinations led me down the path of history and English, but "Merk" could make placing the members of the animal kingdom by phylum, class and order seem important and interesting. He knew best teaching practices long before anyone else had thought of them.

Agriculture proved to be a repeat of the previous year. English and

American history remained among my favorite classes and chorus was similar to band.

In 10th grade I drove Dad's pickup to the homecoming game. While I was stopped at a stop sign near the school, Paul Adamson, a classmate and friend, rammed his dad's pick-up into the back end of mine. Since my truck had a large wooden box for hauling cemetery monuments, Paul's vehicle took the beating. I never bothered to tell Dad about the incident.

11th Grade

Echo High School students rarely held parties in their homes in the 1950's. In the fall of 1956, Diane Syverud, whose father, Bud, experienced a paralyzing wound while fighting in World War II helped us break that tradition. Both Eileen Schwartz and I were invited. Although Eileen's brother, Mel, was my friend, I had never noticed her. That night she caught my attention.

I was the oldest member of my class, but I was naïve about boy-girl relationships. I had dated, but never seriously enough to even kiss a girl. I desired it, but was also apprehensive. The idea of making "the move" and being rejected made my hair stand on end. At Diane's party, I overcame my fears.

I have no idea what served as the catalyst but before the evening was over Eileen and I had found a private place in the Syverud home, where our lips met and I fell head over heels for my pal's kid sister.

School was different after that. I looked forward to seeing Eileen in the hall between classes. We exchanged notes or touched hands. My attention span was limited. My grades slipped. Academics, which had never been the central focus of my life, were less important than ever. Although I wasn't overtly romantic, our relationship was probably too important as part of my life at school.

My romance, however, didn't interfere with the most significant event of the school year, the junior class play, *A Man Called Peter*. Mrs. Olson, the director, was also our chorus director and taught general music. She was a petite, youthful woman who demanded respectful behavior, peak performances and self-motivation. During our first chorus rehearsal, David, a big, troublesome kid who had just moved to Echo, underestimated her. When she assigned him a seat in chorus, he challenged her. "I ain't going to sit in that *cheer*. It's not *comfrtarble*. I like the *cheer* I'm in."

"You're not sitting anywhere in this room buster. Leave immediately."

He started to mutter a response but before he could get out a single word she commanded, "Roger, take that *cheer* that David didn't like."

A week before the performance of our class play Mrs. Olson told Paul Adamson, our lead actor, who was playing the role of Peter Marshall, "Unless you have your lines memorized perfectly by tomorrow I will be replacing you with Gene. He's a quick study and will be ready to perform on opening night." Paul knew she wasn't bluffing and performed flawlessly the next evening. He was superb in the role of the famous pastor.

The week after the play, Mrs. Olson arranged for the cast members to travel in a carpool to Clarkfield, Minn. to see that high school perform *Our Town*. I loaded my 1948 Plymouth with Gene Kissner, Shirley Meier, Joy Arndt and Mel Schwartz. Together with Mr. and Mrs. Olson's carload of students, we traveled forty miles through the cold to see the performance. It was awe inspiring. Although we were proud of our performance, *Our Town* introduced us to a new level of theater. The spare set left the scenery to the audience's imagination allowing us to focus on the interactions of the actors. We were intent on grasping the complex role of the impassive stage manager, with his godlike ability to move the audience through time, place and circumstances. His role added depth to the unfolding drama. The shifting of time from the present to the past revealed lost opportunities by the characters to experience each moment of life more fully. This opportunity to grow intellectually, as we were in the midst of our own self-discovery would not have been provided without Mrs. Olson taking risks, giving freely of her time and being willing to mentor us.

Other 11th grade classes offered minimal academic growth. Miss Anderson, the English teacher, was a certified Spanish teacher. We could take Spanish as an elective in place of agriculture. Dennis Johnson and I were the only members of the class to register for it, so the administration dropped it. I never did study a second language. That was a missed opportunity.

Miss Anderson was a good teacher. We read short stories and a wide variety of literature. Often she called on me to read aloud and frequently commented as Mrs. Hegdahl had, "Roger, you read well.

It's important to read orally with feeling." With her encouragement I made certain I did.

Mr. Sonnechson, the new band director, was dry as a bone, and the music he chose reflected his personality.

The hapless Mr. Busch, who had earlier been driven out by a student rebellion, was vastly superior. Mr. Larsen, our school principal, also taught social studies. He was a humorless tyrant with no enthusiasm for the subject or the students. Mr. Bocko, who taught speech, gave some interesting, creative assignments. One was to type a thirty minute radio program with 30 second commercials, music, and chat time. Had I worked harder in the class it would have been very beneficial to me in my life experiences.

A major influence outside school on my career plans was church. I taught Sunday school, was church custodian and was president of our Luther League youth group my junior and senior year in high school. Both of these positions allowed me to test the waters at being a self-starter and serving the public. Teaching Sunday school introduced me to the difficulties of managing kids. It quickly became evident that if children weren't busy, they were in trouble. I learned too, as custodian, that if the coal burning furnace in the church wasn't fired up early enough on cold winter mornings, the congregation would tell me about it.

The youth group leadership taught me to take charge of a group. Although I had been a member of many school groups, leadership was new to me. Planning of Sunday school activities was a shared exercise with all of the teachers, but I found myself comfortable with leading the lesson alone.

My parents were convinced that our little white church on the prairie taught unfailing moral principles. God had commanded them to require their children to learn and follow those principles. Consequently, they had higher expectations for me in church responsibilities than in the school.

Twelfth Grade

The senior year started with a bang. After the homecoming parade, I was cruising down Main Street in my 1948 Plymouth when I spotted Carol Kvistad, a cute blonde, strutting down the sidewalk. I pulled to the curb and shouted, "Would you like a ride?"

Mel Schwartz, who was driving behind me also moved to the curb but didn't stop. The grill of his Ford rammed into the trunk of my Plymouth. That ended my four year run of homecoming car accidents but didn't end my senior year foolishness.

It sometimes seemed as though many of us used the year to hide our true character. We "borrowed" watermelons and cantaloupe from local gardens and ate them for lunch at a picnic off the school grounds the following day. We moved our agriculture teacher's car from its parking place by the school and left it parked on Main Street downtown. We took the tires off Mr. Bocko's car during his class play rehearsal and left the car sitting on blocks. We threw a cantaloupe on

Mr. Schoen's roof while he and his wife were entertaining guests. I am pleased that I planned none of these things nor was I a major participant in any of them, but I was always present. Oddly, none of these acts of mischief were committed out of anger toward the victim.

As my senior school year ended, there were choices that had to be made. A recruiter from DeVry Technical Institute in Chicago, Ill., founded by former heavyweight boxing world champion; Jack Dempsey, invited the senior boys to listen to his pitch. Even though it would have freed me from English class, I chose not to attend. My good friends Arden Bendix, Gene Kissner, Paul Adamson and Mel Schwartz all attended and decided to hang their future on what they heard. They tried to persuade me to reconsider but I never did. I believed teaching school would be a better way to make a living. If our basketball coach and English teacher, Leo Murphy, could do it, I knew I could too. With only enough money to attend one quarter, and a great deal of faith, I sent $10.00 and an application to enroll at Mankato State College.

May 26, 1958, the evening of our graduation my friend and classmate was struck with adversity that would have destroyed a lesser person. He suffered a psychotic break. Events foretelling it, in hindsight, were probably obvious, but no one put the clues together to figure out what was happening. He had experienced significant behavioral changes during our senior year. He had changed from the serious, scholarly, shy, student athlete to the class clown. He goaded teachers by setting off dud firecrackers in class and slipping out the window while another teacher's back was turned.

While the rest of the class wondered about what came after graduation, his choices for the immediate future were made for him. The rest of us moved timidly in the direction of our choice while he needed time and therapy before he could advance at all.

Ironically, one of our most ineffective teachers played a major role in sparking my interest in teaching English. The first semester our English class, taught by Mr. Murphy, was a joke. Students arm wrestled, pulled fingers and generally "horsed around" every day. Murphy often joined in the foolishness. For some reason he decided to teach the second semester. He prepared a packet of study questions on *Macbeth* and, like it or not, we read and studied Shakespeare. The abrupt change caused a mutiny. When it was finished Captain Murphy, stood firmly on the deck as Gordie Oie struggled in his swim back to the ship. I loved the work and found Shakespearian literature meaningful and pleasurable. I can still recite; from memory; passages from *Macbeth*. Most of my other classes, including social studies, physics, and agriculture, were dull. I might have enjoyed physics more; if I had mastered the fundamentals of algebra in ninth grade.

Psychology was my favorite class that year. Mrs. Nelson, from Redwood Falls, returned to teaching after a long hiatus to raise her daughter. She challenged us to understand the basis for human behavior and held us accountable in demonstrating an understanding of the concepts she taught. For a while I considered counseling as a career.

The Support Staff

While teachers are responsible for providing students with opportunities to obtain the skills required to succeed. The school secretaries, cooks, janitors and bus drivers also play roles in the network connecting the school to the community. They are often the nurturers and disciplinarians in situations that fall outside the teacher's area of responsibility.

Our school secretary, my Aunt Minnie Lecy, was the first hurdle in the administrative offices. If students sought an excused absence or permission to use their car they first talked to her. She decided whether perusal by the next level of authority was warranted. Minnie had the heartiest laugh of anyone in Yellow Medicine County, and she offered it up freely at appropriate moments. Whether they got the approval they sought or not, she offered them the gift of her laughter. Students nearly always left the office with a "Minnie moment" they could share with friends.

Harry Pullen, a trusted friend, was the school custodian through my junior year. When he caught us playing cards on the floor in the bathroom during study hall, he warned us of future consequences, but didn't snitch.

During my senior year, Dad became the new custodian. At first this concerned me. Dad would become an omnipresent figure in my life. There were times when I preferred to be out of his sight. Sometimes my friends and I played hoops when the school was closed. We placed a small rock between the entrance door and the doors casing. It prevented the door from locking and enabled us admittance whenever we wanted. With Dad present in the school the risk might be greater than the reward.

As it turned out Dad's presence was a positive. I benefited financially when he hired me to remove the cinders left from the coal-burning furnace. I shot buckets when he worked in the building on Saturday mornings. When I forgot something at school, he could let me in.

The school cooks, Mrs. Oie and Mrs. Dahl, although not trained in psychology, understood and applied Pavlovian conditioning. Daily they used food as a tool to control our behavior. Simply by asking, "Hey, Roger, could you use another slice of bread?" They earned my loyalty and got from me the lunchroom behavior they wanted. I still have vivid memories of their smiling faces dishing up food.

What Worked–What Didn't

During the 13 years I attended Echo Public Schools I had 26 different teachers. While most of them did their job a well, a few struggled and a few excelled. Those who excelled had varied teaching styles, but the commonalities were striking. Today the skills they had have been classified into categories and labeled best practices. Although we didn't label their practices then, we recognized that they were doing something special.

Perception is not absolute truth, but it motivates behavior. My perception that Mrs. Hegdahl considered me one of her better fifth grade students drove me to seek that status in her class, just as my perception that my first grade teacher considered me to be an immature, undisciplined six year old encouraged me to prove her correct. I believe both teachers were dedicated and wanted me to achieve the skills needed for that stage of my development, but the tools they used were quite different. The hammer was less effective in helping me succeed in 1st grade than the sand paper used to smooth my rough edges in 5th grade.

Communication with parents was far more difficult for teachers in the 1940's than now. Teachers today share concerns about students' progress with parents via the computer, and solutions for problems are often cooperatively sought. In the 1940's we didn't even have a telephone. Teachers worked in isolation from parents and received little or no assistance from school leaders in resolving the problems they confronted.

Bud Christianson, the music man, Tom MrKonich, the biology teacher and football coach, Mrs. Olson, the music teacher and play director and Mrs. Hegdahl, my fifth grade teacher overcame those communication issues by careful planning. Each had clear goals. Their classes held no surprises. Students memorized, practiced solved and grasped the concepts in sequence. They understood that knowledge is sequential and that missing a piece of the sequence doomed future learning.

At appropriate times they all had senses of humor. Their students were able to find joy in learning. All demanded that we succeed and found pleasure in our accomplishments. They challenged students to reach the pinnacle of their abilities. They recognized that like flowers, each student needed differing amounts of sunshine, water and fertilizer and they knew when to provide them. They recognized their classroom wasn't the center of their student's world and coached, attended and participated in their student's other school activities. Words of encouragement and praise flowed freely from them to students who achieved success in those activities. They also expressed disappointment to students who breached their code of conduct. These were the teachers I hoped to emulate when I considered a teaching career.

Despite the inauspicious beginning, education has been the driving force of my adult life. Good fortune, moderate risk taking, preparation and good luck have all afforded me the opportunity to serve in education as a teacher, administrator and school board member. These experiences were gratifying and fulfilling beyond my greatest expectations. They helped clarify my perception of how an educational program might achieve its maximum potential. In spite of my rough start that goal drove my adult life in school.

What I Learned and What I Didn't

My high school diploma education states, "This student has satisfactorily completed the requirements for graduation from Echo High School." Having maintained a "B" average in grades nine through twelve, I was even considered an honor student. I had learned a great deal during my twelve years, but my academic accomplishments didn't warrant being honored for them.

After 16,380 hours of attending classes in the Echo school system I couldn't locate the majority of the 50 states in the United States or the majority of countries in the world on a map; I didn't know a verb from a noun or a subject from a predicate; I couldn't solve a math problem that asked me to determine an unknown number; I didn't know where to begin or end each paragraph while writing a composition; I didn't know what a Jim Crow law was; I couldn't explain what caused World War II; I had no understanding of how propaganda could be used to twist the truth; My extra-curricular reading had been limited to a couple biographies and novels, and I had never studied for an exam. I had several pages missing in my book of knowledge.

I had some noteworthy accomplishments that were worthy of pride. I had learned to deal with disappointment when I failed to become a regular player on the basketball team; I had scored in the ninety plus percentile in both reading and basic math skills on the Iowa Basic Skills tests; I had discovered that I enjoyed reading and analyzing Shakespeare, and committing the details of historical events to memory was easy for me. Although not talented, I enjoyed performing in plays, band, and chorus. Probably most importantly, I loved the social experiences that schools offered.

Weighing the plusses and the minuses of my resume, I believed I would find teaching to be a fulfilling career.

How to Improve

While my school experience was superior in some aspects, it failed in others. Dr. William Schmidt's study in the 1990's clarified some of the age old failures of American education. Most of his findings should not have been a surprise. They were evident even in the 1940's and 50's. There is a common body of knowledge that is required for successful living. That body of knowledge must be acquired by youth at appropriate learning stages in their lives. This happens only when curriculum clearly dictates it. Teachers must monitor each student's progress on the body of knowledge for which they are responsible and reteach students who do not master the core curriculum. Fifth grade students, for example, must be able to identify the fifty states. Students, parents, teachers and administrators must understand this and agree to serve as partners in achieving it.

When I was a public school student The Iowa Basic Skills Tests were administered. It appears they were not utilized as tools to monitor individual progress but rather as guidelines for the district. I recall being told, "Your class is a good class." This statement was partially based on the results of the basic standards test. I never was told "You must learn to locate the forty-eight states on a map" as a result of that test or any other test.

Dr. Schmidt, one of the current gurus of comparative educational testing said, "The curriculum in American schools is a mile wide and an inch deep. Students must achieve mastery of the core requirements of the curriculum." In spite of the fact that I learned a great deal in Echo, I failed the basic requirements which Schmidt referenced.

The Changing School Culture

When our forefathers set aside a section of land from every township to provide for public education in the Northwest Ordinance of 1787, they planned to provide enough education to meet the needs of an agrarian society. Reading, writing and arithmetic were all that was considered necessary.

When it comes to change there is always a cultural lag. People hold on to outdated thinking and practices. In *The Sabre Tooth Curriculum* the author, Abner Peddiwell, details how early man continued to teach children how to kill sabre toothed tigers long after they were extinct. Teachers had taught them the skill, so naturally their children must also learn it. That is why all Echo boys had to take Agriculture.

Over time, we became more holistic in our view of education, and the role of extracurricular became overly valued. It grew in popularity in the 1940's and 1950's and became so deeply woven into the school culture that many believed it was equal to or greater than the academic curriculum. Separating the impact of academic and extra-curricular activities on the lives of students is difficult, but it must be done to measure the effects on academic achievement. Achieving satisfactory results in core curriculum is the foremost responsibility of schools.

Transition to College

In Echo the pool hall was the center of the men's social activity. The building, an old, stucco structure, was long, narrow and leaning. Upon entering, one's first glance revealed a single, large room with three marred wooden booths on the middle of the west wall. A sturdy, walnut bar stood out three feet off the east wall. A long, brass foot rail ran almost half the length of the building, along the bottom of the bar. Near the center of the room were three wooden card tables, each surrounded by four high-back chairs. In the back were two slate pool tables with leather pockets that made a snapping noise when pool balls with significant velocity slapped against them. The 4x4 toilet enclosure contained no sink and the toilet was rarely flushed and even more rarely cleaned. This place was the norm in my youth. I was about to experience culture shock.

During high school I spent many of my most enjoyable evenings in this dilapidated old building. My friends and I gave each other nicknames there. Gordie Oie, who was a bit of a klutz, we called Dainty; his brother Dick, always luckier at pool than he was skilled, became Stink; Mel Schwartz, six foot four, and wearing size 15 shoes, was Sloughfoot. Here we all had argued furiously over plays in games of Euchre, Smear and Whist. We had shared and exaggerated romantic escapades. This was the center of our little universe. But on September 3, 1958, Bud Herberg, the dapper, moustached proprietor and I were its only occupants. I had never been lonelier.

Early that morning three of my best buddies Gene Kissner, Mel Schwartz and Paul Adamson had left for Chicago to attend a technical college. Other pals Hib Hackbarth and Carlyle Kaaz had left a few weeks before to complete basic training at Fort Riley, Kansas.

Was life as I had known and enjoyed it over?

That summer had been nearly perfect. We all had found jobs doing farm labor, construction, and carpentry. The work was taxing but we recovered quickly from it. We enjoyed late, revelry filled evenings and still performed our work admirably.

Now, everything had changed and I wasn't at all confident I was ready for it. The realization of what was happening frightened and saddened me. The awareness that it was time to leave Echo hung heavily on my heart. I left the pool hall to think about my new life.

I had saved $370.00 from wages earned during that summer. Of that, I needed to pay two debts before I left town. I owed Irvin Pederson, the proprietor of the *Hurry Back Inn*, forty dollars for hamburgers, cherry cokes, and butterscotch sundaes. My other debt was to Harold Meier, the owner of the Pure Oil station in town. I had charged thirty dollars for gasoline and used tires. That left me with three hundred dollars and change to start college.

Ready; or not, I left for Mankato State College on September 11th with $5.00 in my billfold and enough money to pay tuition, dormitory fees and textbook expenses. Since Dad's 1949 Ford pickup wouldn't work for our trip, Grandpa Stoufer drove me to Mankato in his 1956 Ford Galaxy and Dad rode along. At 3 p.m. I said goodbye to my most ardent fan, Mom, and waved to my kid sisters.

The trip to Mankato seemed to last an eternity but finally we pulled into the parking lot of my new home, Searing Center, the men's dormitory. My first thought upon seeing it was, I bet there are pool and card tables in there.

NOTEBOOK ERA

Mankato State College 1958-1962

Introduction to College Life

It's time to leave
my father said,
your sister Susan
needs your bed.

Dad and Grandpa said a quick goodbye to me in the parking lot outside Searing Center and abandoned me. Ma Eby, the resident supervisor at Searing, stood behind a U-shaped counter that served as a front desk. After gathering the necessary information and collecting my rent for the quarter, she handed me a packet of information, my keys to room 320 and sent me on my way.

When I entered my new room, I was *underwhelmed* by its plainness. There was a green sink attached to the white block walls to my immediate right and a walled area with a clothes bar to my left. Beyond were two tiny single beds clinging to the walls on both sides of the room. Tucked tightly in the back were two – three foot rectangular combination desks with drawers for clothing and chairs that slid under the desktops. In the center of the rear wall was a small window overlooking Glenwood Avenue below. The room was perfectly symmetrical and, unlike the Echo pool hall, totally lacking in personality.

A few clothes were hanging on the clothes bar and a small suitcase on the floor beneath them indicated that my roommate, whoever he was, had arrived before me. I hung my meager amount of clothing, placed my toiletries on the shelf by the sink, and put my underclothing in the drawers that were left empty, and in five minutes was settled in my new home.

I sat down to relax, hoping my roommate would soon return. Quickly growing restless, I decided to reconnoiter and see what else Searing had to offer. Returning to the lobby, I found a comfortable chair and located a copy of a newspaper called *The Free Press*. It surprised me a bit that the newspaper didn't charge a fee for a subscription but I concluded that maybe it survived on its advertising income. Finding nothing of interest in the paper and feeling uncomfortable sitting alone in the lobby, I decided to continue my exploration and ventured down the stairway to Searing's lower level.

There I found what I was seeking. To the right was a television room with about thirty chairs lined in rows. Straight ahead was another room with a pool table, card tables and chairs. Two of the tables were occupied by guys playing cards. I walked over to them hoping to strike up a conversation. When that didn't happen, I watched the card game for a few minutes, and since none of the players paid attention to me, I returned to my room, where I lay down on the bed and waited again for my "roommate."

At 10:30 p.m. a key rattled in the door, and in he strolled. He was a couple of inches taller than me, and about 15 pounds lighter and was carrying a curved case that obviously held a musical instrument.

I quickly blurted out, "Hi, I'm Roger Stoufer. I guess you're my roommate."

He responded. "I'm Art Welter. I've been at the Newman Center playing my guitar and singing some Johnny Cash. Do you like his music?'

It didn't take me two seconds to put my foot in my mouth. "No, I guess I'm more of a Buddy Holly fan. "Peggy Sue" and "Rave On" are my favorites."

He opened his guitar case, sat down on his bed, and presented me with his best, "Folsum Prison Blues."

"Buddy Holly can't come close to that," he said after he finished singing. He then broke into "I Keeep a Close Watch on this Heart of Mine."

"Oh my God," I thought. "This could be a long year."

Registration, Physicals and Friday Afternoon Classes

The packet that Ma Eby had given me contained a schedule of events for the orientation for freshmen. Various tests were scheduled. These were designed to assist students in selecting majors and minors that matched their aptitude. Social activities that included mixers like dances and game night were also planned. Purple and gold beanies were included in the packet. Freshmen were to wear these from "rise and shine" to "collapse" into bed for the next three days. This was part of a mind control propaganda program designed by administrators to shift new students allegiances and loyalties completely to Mankato State College.

Monday morning, after my first meal of Slater slop in the cafeteria (Slater food service provided the meals for the college), I slipped on my Echo High School letter jacket and headed for Old Main, where Dr. Schwartz, the men's dean, was to explain our new role as college students. I walked alone, as Art had arranged to be with his new friends from the Newman Center and quickly ditched me.

Leaving Searing, I was abruptly stopped by two authoritative guys who accosted me with, "High school letter jackets aren't worn on campus. You're a Mankato State College student now. You wear purple and gold here. Get that red and black off."

Shocked and angered, I ignored them and kept on walking toward Old Main.

The remainder of the day consisted of some meetings and completing

48

standardized tests. That evening, though, was noteworthy. All new students took their college physicals in the health and physical education building. When we arrived we were given a form to fill out. We completed the standard fields for name and address and the doctors completed the health information section after their brief review of our bodies. We moved from one station to the next like hogs in a slaughter house. The first station was dental.

The line there was short and I moved quickly to an open chair, where I sat down and was immediately confronted by some old dude wearing a white coat. He took my form and said, "Roger Stauffer." Without hesitating long enough for me to correct the mispronunciation of my name he continued, "Open your mouth." He dug around for a few seconds with some tools, wrote a few things on my form and sent me on to the hernia doctor. On my way, I read the on the form "imperfect occlusion." Not knowing the meaning of occlusion, I decided I had a serious tooth disease.

There were two lines for the hernia station. I chose the shorter one which turned out to be a painful mistake. The old doctor had me drop my drawers, and before I could prepare myself, he grabbed my left testicle, squeezed it, and pushed his finger almost through my pelvis. I yelped like a wounded puppy, but that didn't sensitize him. He promptly pursued the right testicle, again doubling me over with discomfort.

As I limped away, I met a kid I'd talked to in the dental line. He whispered, "Good God! Didn't anybody warn you about that old sadist?"

Nobody seemed to know why we had those physicals but the following day was class registration and I would have been willing to endure six of them to avoid that.

That first registration proved to be the most miserable experience I had in my four years of college. We formed a line outside a large room in Old Main. It might once have been a library. There were no assigned times to arrive, only opening and closing hours. The early birds registered first and filled the classes. Not being one of them, my wait to register lasted over an hour.

I had studied the catalogue of classes and selected courses in history, English, sociology, political science and physical education, all of which gave me a chance of academic success. Professors seated at tables handed out admit cards to students who wished to register for their class. I hadn't been told that there was a limited number of cards and assumed that when I reached the front of a line, I would be given a card for a class. Repeatedly as I reached the front of lines, I was informed the class had been filled. After an hour and a half, I held one class card and was considering hitchhiking back to Echo where nobody ever registered for a class. There we were told what we would take. This was crap.

The hour for closing registration was fast approaching, and the registration room was emptying of students. I was registered for four credits. Taking the bull by the horns, I approached professors who had denied me cards earlier and appealed my case. This approach enabled me to secure all the classes I wanted but English. Dr. Roy Meyer was still at his post, and I pleaded with him for permission to register for his freshman 174 composition class. After some hesitation, he allowed me to enter a class that met at 3 p.m. on Tuesday, Thursday and Friday. Upon completion of registration my head pounded, my thoughts raced and my doubts about ever becoming a Joe College had increased dramatically.

The Academics

Being short on money I decided to rent rather than purchase my textbooks. I was unable to locate rentals for music appreciation and sociology so I attended and took copious notes for both of those classes and hoped that would suffice. My band and chorus experience in high school helped in music appreciation and at mid-term I earned a C on Dr. Epple's midterm exam.

Dr. White taught sociology and wasn't quite as generous. She marked our progress after two weeks of class with an exam. When she returned it, only three students in a class of 30 had earned a C. She warned the rest of us "Unless you pick up the pace in this class, you'll be packing your suitcases in Mankato." She then told the students who had failed to leave the room immediately, while those who passed were allowed to stay. As we left she said, "Spend the next hour in the library reading and understanding the material in chapter 4." Although I was unnerved by this, I didn't buy a book but tried to improve on my listening and note-taking. At the end of the quarter I received a B.

My other grades were all C's. With no resources to finance the following quarter, I considered dropping out of college anyhow. But upon my arrival home the week before the end of the quarter mom met me at the door with a smile. "I visited Leonard Nelson at the bank and he's willing to make us a two-hundred-fifty dollar loan for you to attend school next quarter."

This news was overwhelming. Dad did the little banking that our family needed. Mom was too shy and sensitive. She had reached far beyond her comfort zone to do this. Because of her intervention, I was about to become a second-quarter freshman. I decided to settle in and make friends.

Although Art, and I never bonded, I had found commonalities with several guys from Milroy, Tracy and Walnut Grove, and was anxious to continue with college and to grow those friendships. None of my new friends, though, had fared as well with their grades as I had with their first quarter, so we all decided to dedicate ourselves to becoming better scholars.

I purchased or rented textbooks for all of my classes the second quarter and bought a separate notebook for each class. As a third step to achieve better grades, I spent evenings studying in the library. A requirement of English 175 was to write a research paper. Miss Hunt, the professor, warned us immediately of the dangers of choosing a research topic too broad in scope. Ignoring her advice, I chose to write on the life of Mary Todd Lincoln. Although the research was helpful and the ibid's and opcit's fell into place, the vastness of the topic prevented me from researching anything beyond biographical data. Good efforts notwithstanding, I earned a C.

My research skills weren't much honed but my interest in truth seeking was considerably greater. A major sources for my paper was a biography on the Lincolns written by Lincoln's law partner in Illinois, William Herndon. His account of Mary made Jezebel, the biblical— "queen of mean,"—seem saintly in comparison. Doubting some of the account about Mary, I read sources on Herndon that detailed their sour relationship, which likely explained his harsh account.

Dr. Winston Benson's political science class was my favorite class and he was my favorite professor. In addition to the textbook assignments we were accountable for all of the information in *Newsweek*. Every Wednesday Dr. Benson drilled us on current affairs. Fidel Castro was then making his move to overthrow Juan Batista in Cuba. Dr. Benson read widely on the subject and added more insight than was offered by *Newsweek*. He piqued our curiosity and encouraged us to seek information from various current sources. To this day newspapers and news magazines continue to serve as an indispensible tool for me in my search for political truth and understanding.

My other classes that quarter, including art appreciation, chemistry, and health were required stumbling blocks to avoid tripping on; as I advanced toward a major. They broadened my base of knowledge but they never turned my crank to start my engine.

In March 1959, broke and owing two-hundred-fifty dollars to the Citizens State Bank in Echo, I dropped out of college, returned home and sought employment. My friends Dick and Gordie Oie were also job seeking. Together we hooked up with the E. J. Clinton pole barn company. Our first assignment was to build a huge barn outside of

Sleepy Eye. The poles were already in the ground and our job was to frame and roof the structure.

The rest of the crew was "older." They were in their 20's and 30's and had worked in the building industry for some time. They worked sunup to sundown and then drank cheap booze until the bar closed. Dick, Gordie, and I were complete misfits. We lacked the necessary work and social skills to survive long in their environment.

My sister, Faye, removed me from this hell by securing me a position on the assembly line at Schaefer's refrigeration on Eighth Street and Washington Avenue in Minneapolis—the heart of the ghetto in 1959. Pawn shops were the dominant retail outlets, and alcoholics and panhandlers the governing population.

My job consisted of crating the completed commercial freezers or cleaning them before they were crated. Most Schaefer employees were Mexicans. The boss, Louis, was a good guy who was intolerant of idle hands but loved to laugh. Although he spoke some English, he preferred Spanish or Tex-Mex. Our eight-hour workday began at 7:00 a.m. and concluded at 3:30 p.m. When possible, I would go the bathroom at 3 p.m. to wash my hands and face on company time. As I left the work area, Louis would say something in Spanish, part of which sounded like "Poinetta."

The Mexicans standing in the area would roar with laughter, so I would join them. One day I asked my working partner, Juan, to translate what Louis was saying. He smiled, "He's saying, you going to jack off again?" That ended my company time clean-up.

I first lived alone in a rented room located near Excelsior Boulevard, a couple of blocks west of Warren Cadillac and a few blocks south of the Munsingwear building. I paid $10.00 a week for a room with a tiny, white refrigerator, a gas burning camp stove, a metal bed, a straight-back wooden chair and a white wooden table large enough to accommodate only two chairs.

For one month this room was the center of my life. I left for work at 6 a.m., took the city bus east on Hennepin Avenue to Washington Avenue, and walked eight blocks north on Washington to the site of the Schaefer factory, where I punched my time clock, and carted commercial refrigerators for the next eight hours. I walked down Washington because I never could figure out how to transfer from one bus to another without purchasing a second ticket.

Dad, who was the school custodian in Echo, understood the loneliness I was experiencing and discussed it with Mr. Bocko, my high school speech teacher. As a student at the University of Minnesota, Mr. Bocko had lived in a rooming house on Emerson Avenue, where he had been served an evening meal, provided a private room, and offered companionship with other young men in circumstances similar to his own. While still maintaining my budget, I was able to improve my living conditions by moving to his former residence. Ma Soley, a woman in her late 70's, proved to be a caring and generous landlady. I planned to spend my entire summer there but after I had been there slightly over a month Paul Sebey and Gordon Pederson, two high school friends, found employment at Schaefer's. Together we rented a small apartment in St. Paul and used Gordie's car for our transportation needs.

By September 1959 I had repaid my loan and saved enough money to return to college. It appeared that if I budgeted carefully, found a part-time job to supplement my savings and lived off campus, I would be able to attend school the whole 1959-1960 academic year. I also discovered I would have new roommates.

After a year of struggling with his life, D, a high school classmate and friend was ready to move forward with his life. Roy, the captain of our football team my sophomore year in high school, had completed his hitch in the military and was also planning to attend college. The three of us found a big, old house on 712 Warren Street atop the river valley about a mile from the campus. The first floor was occupied by the Beckers, a family with two small children. The second and third floors each had four two-bed, bedrooms, a bath and a kitchen. The couple living on the first floor managed the building and supervised the sixteen male students who occupied these rooms. This was home for my sophomore year in college. My high school friends shared a room and I bunked with senior music major, Roger Young. I rarely saw him as he was in love and at a different stage in life than I was.

I showed my friends the ropes and we completed our registration the opening day of school. By then it had become routine. Focusing on the required courses I still needed, I took basic mathematics, Greek mythology, physics, geography and some gym classes.

The only class that quarter that drew my interest was Greek mythology, taught by Dr. Norman Adams. He had a strong, Southern drawl and a deep, resonant voice that added mesmerizing depth to *The Odyssey* as he read it aloud. I listened to the drama unfold as Dr.

Adams read of how Odysseus strapped himself to the mast of the ship so he wouldn't succumb to the destructive lure of the sirens' beautiful voices. "My God," I thought, "that is the temptation all heroic, successful men must face." I wondered how many broke loose from the mast and sailed to their destruction.

As I read from *The Odyssey* while sitting in the library, I wondered where my journey might take me. Certainly it would not contain the intrigue, and danger that Odysseus had faced. But I, too, hoped to see the world and to be seduced by its beauty and attractions.

After the end of each quarter, grade slips were mailed home to parents. My mother, who believed a "C" was an average grade, was ecstatic about my performance that quarter. She told everyone that I was considerably above average in my scholarship as I began my sophomore year in college holding a respectable 2.4 grade point average. Although Mom was satisfied, I was disappointed in my grade from Dr. Adams. The syllabus indicated that students would have four exams in his class, with each grade to be weighted equally. I had earned two B's and an A coming into the final exam and felt assured of a B for the quarter. When my grade slip was mailed home, it showed a C. Crushed and angry, but still at heart the kid who dared not ask the Minneapolis bus driver how to transfer, I accepted the seeming injustice without question.

My roommate, Roy, earned a mix of "B"s and "C"s but D, my other roomie, received a "D" in zoology. In his zeal to complete his first crazed registration, D failed to notice the course had a biology prerequisite. I feared the consequences of the D more than he did, as he enrolled for zoology II the next quarter.

In addition to the grade problem D had trouble adjusting to the crowded, sometimes combative living conditions in our home on Warren Street. He relaxed by playing his accordion and sometimes cranked it up after 10:00 p.m. This was met with threats, both from the fifteen students packed into this sardine can, and also from the young couple downstairs who were raising two small children.

The mile-long, downhill walk to the campus, which had been pleasant in the fall, became treacherous during the dark and icy days of winter. I usually walked for my 8 a.m. class and stayed for the rest of the day.

I had selected history as my major and enrolled in Dr. Tom Moir's European history class. Dr. Moir, tall, thin and mustached, wore thick glasses and always carried a pocket watch attached to his slacks with a gold chain. He opened every class with the same regimen—pulling his watch from his pocket, and placing it carefully on the center of his desk, clearing his throat twice and beginning his lecture at the precise point where he had finished the day before.

Dr. Moir, when confronted by the administration for giving no A's to students was reputed to have responded, "When a student earns an A in my class, he/she will be awarded one. Until then, I will continue with my current practice."

He gave all essay exams and demanded detailed explanations. If an event was historically significant, students were expected to explain, for example, how the design of the ships in the Spanish Armada affected the Armada's defeat in 1588." He taught his students that the "devil" was always in the details and that making arguments without using supporting details was futile. Incorporating that in my teaching and life later helped me to be a more effective instructor.

That quarter I hit the books with an intensity that I didn't even know I was capable of and earned an "A" from Dr. Moir. The rest of my grades were "B"s which placed me in the top half of my class. Considering my weak start in education I was pleased as punch with myself.

Spring quarter I enrolled in eighteen credits and finished with a "B" average. My advisor, Dr. Cyril Allen, who was drier than an ear of corn in October, taught two of my classes. I earned an A in each of them. By the the end of my sophomore year I had become a bona fide student. It appeared I might graduate in four years after all, despite my lack of financial resources, but to do this I desperately needed a summer job that paid well and started immediately.

The national economy in the spring of 1960 was weak and jobs were nearly impossible to find. The rural areas had been hit the hardest, so I decided to crash with some high school buddies who were working at Honeywell in Minneapolis and living in a large rental house on 1309 West Franklin. Gene Kissner, Mel Schwartz, Paul Adamson, Chuck Skaarstad, and Marv Alvheim let me stay rent free while I sought a job. Marv, too, was unemployed, so each morning we struck out together to find work. Each evening we promised the other guys that the next day we'd either find "a job or a jar." For several weeks they roared with laughter when they returned home and saw us gulping beer.

Marv and I decided that since there were no jobs, we'd enlist in the

Army and ride it out there until better economic times returned. We met with a recruiter and made an appointment to return the next day to sign on the dotted line.

But once again Faye came through for me when she called that afternoon and announced, "one of the guys who works with Newt quit, and they're looking for someone to park cars at the Foshay. Come stay with us tonight and go to work with Newt tomorrow."

The next morning, Newt Crom, Faye's husband, introduced me to his boss, Wally Chambers, who was soon to be my boss too. Wally was a balding black man in his sixties with a warm smile and a comfortable demeanor that were endearing.

Following a brief interview he hired me saying with a smile "You'll find I'm no Simon Legree."

The job was simple. I was to park cars and retrieve them for the business people who owned or rented spaces in the Foshay, the tallest, most prestigious office building in Minneapolis. The cars were parked below street level in the basement. As tenants arrived or left, four parking attendants were available to park or retrieve their cars. With over 100 parking stalls, it took some time to learn where to locate the cars. Customers disliked waiting, so attendants hustled up or down the narrow staircase that led to the lower levels. We were also required to memorize the make and model of each customer's car, because it was embarrassing to the attendant and upsetting to the customer if the wrong car was delivered. The rush hours were from 7:30 to 10:30 a.m. and 3:30 to 5:30 p.m. The intervening time was usually slow and allowed for socialization.

The Foshay was built in the 1930's and the parking stalls were designed for Model A's not 1960 Cadillacs. The cars had to be squeezed carefully into the small stalls. Customers grew angry if they noticed scratches or dents on their shiny, new cars. The pressure made me anxious, but I soon learned to jump in the car, turn the key, throw the shift lever into drive, squeal the tires and put the hammer down, making certain I honked the horn as I roared up the single-lane, curved ramp that accommodated both up and down traffic. Time flew during the rush and it was exciting.

Most customers had no interest in developing any relationship with the attendants who parked their cars, but others were personable. Charlie Horn, the owner of Federal Cartridge Corporation, was one of those.

He was about sixty, six feet tall and white-haired. Every day he wore a fresh, white carnation in the lapel of his suit. He loved to tease and often shared his life experiences. Once he said, "I hate those damn symphony orchestra concerts, but my wife enjoys them. I guess I'll just keep my mouth shut and go tonight." Charlie rented three spaces for his shiny new Caddys, but never drove them. His chauffer, Rick, did.

Rick lived with the Horns and was about Charlie's age and size except Rick had a Santa Claus belly. He always wore a dark-blue suit, white shirt and navy necktie. I marveled at how his shirts stretched skin tight across his body and wondered whether they were tailor made to do that. Rick waited for Charlie in the parking ramp, where he read the newspaper and told us anecdotes of his son, his youth and his wilder days. He befriended me and called me "Little Sir Echo" in reference to my size and my hometown.

Rick's son, an English professor at Oxford University, had published a book on the life of Shakespeare. When Rick learned I was an English minor, he gave me a copy. Although Rick took great pride in his son, their relationship was strained by Ricks's divorce from his mother.

Once Rick confided that he "ran booze" during the Depression. He never revealed whether Charlie had been one of his customers. He left that to my imagination.

My favorite Rick moment came when he confronted Fred Fadell, another client. He was a top executive of Sister Kenny, a charitable organization with a world-renowned reputation for its treatment of polio. Fred had been accused of embezzling large sums from Sister Kenny. One morning a front page story in the Minneapolis announced Fred's indictment. When Fred opened the door to exit his car, Rick met him with a smile, held up a copy of the *Tribune* and said, "Good morning, Fred. Nice picture of you in the morning paper."

Curious, I watched Fred's eyes. They showed neither a flicker of anger or remorse. He was cool.

I was unique on the staff. All of them, with the exception of Newt, Faye's husband, were African American. All were older, in their late twenties or early thirties. James Elliot, Stan Reese and Brother Barry were longtime employees and knew all the customers by name. Some of the customers were curiouis about me and asked questions.

John Kinnard, a stockbroker who led a firm in the Foshay, was interested in my status as a student at Mankato State. He regularly entered drag races at the airport in Mankato and often bragged to me about his conquests there. Neil Croonquist, an avid golfer, spoke fondly of the Mankato Golf Club. Harry Fisher had a son about my age attending college. He sold me a 1951 Chevrolet at a bargain price. I drove it awhile and then sold it to my cousin, Jimmie Lecy. I used the profit to assist in my college expenses.

Most of the clients were polite but disinterested. My knowledge of a world vastly different than mine in Echo, grew by leaps and bounds as I visited with Rick and the other parking attendants.

A Mr. McNess, a quiet, handsome black man shared very little of his life with anyone. I knew he was married and had a child, because they occasionally visited our work site. Once, after he had been drinking, Newt told me that Jimmy was "pimping" for a girl who sometimes stopped at the Foshay to visit with him. Newt and Jimmie often drank together. Once they both came to work looking like they had spent 15 rounds in the ring with heavyweight champion, Floyd Patterson.

Stan was about Jimmy's age but far more gregarious. Although married with three children, he spent much of his time detailing his sexual exploits with other women. He knew I was inexperienced and likely enjoyed shocking me with his playboy tales. When he revealed his romance with one of our client's wives, I doubted the validity of the tale. To my surprise, one day she appeared in her husband's car and they disappeared into the solitude of the lower levels of the building. In about half an hour they reappeared and Stan added a new story to his repertoire.

Brother Barry, the night attendant, reported for work at 3 p.m. He helped with the afternoon rush and kept the ramp open until midnight. He was the most likable member of our crew. He had a deep, melodious laugh which he shared generously. It might have come to him easily, because he was almost always a little bit drunk. His drink of choice was Silver Satin. Bottles of it were hidden all around the parking area. He once told me, "Roger, no matter how drunk I am when I leave here, I can find my way home; if I can see the Tower."

My brother-in-law was also an alcoholic. A big, handsome guy, who resembled the Western, movie star, Rory Calhoun, he frequently confided in me his dreams of a better life. Although his childhood had been marred by the effects of poverty, he still loved those Northern woods where he had spent his youth. He frequently said, "As soon as I save a little money, Faye and I are going to buy a Christmas tree farm up north and start our new life." For awhile he attended AA meetings, hoping to tie a rope to his dream, but the rope wasn't strong enough and it broke. The demon, alcohol, was always too irresistible to him. His fate was inevitable.

Within months of my return to college Newt was paralyzed in an automobile accident while driving drunk.

Despite the wide cultural gaps that existed between me and my fellow employees, they never demeaned me or saw me as an alien who didn't belong in their world. They encouraged me to find a better life than they had had. When I saved enough money to return to Mankato State, Wally called me into his office and said, "Roger, if you don't have enough money to complete your college and need a job again, call me. As long as I'm working here, you'll be hired back. Good luck." A year later I accepted his offer. My Foshay job broadened my horizons and paid for my bachelor's degree at Mankato State College. For that I am forever grateful.

I Return to College

Registration at college opened two weeks before classes began. By now I had recognized its importance and hoped to avoid taking the leftover classes by registering early. The two problems facing me to accomplish registration were first, I needed a day off work and second a ride to Mankato. Both problems were resolved easily when Wally offered me the day off from work and my buddy; Marv; offered to transport me.

Marv had heard of one of my high school exploits, hauling a load of kids to South Dakota in my 1948 Plymouth and driving the whole way in second-gear overdrive. He decided to match the feat by taking me to Mankato in his 1959 Chevrolet Impala in second-gear overdrive. The ride was swift, registration successful, and the celebration upon our return to Minneapolis was boisterous.

Two weeks later I was a college student again. Roy and D had found an apartment in the basement of a house on 742 Park Avenue in North Mankato. We were nearly three miles from the campus but I still owned the 1951 Chevrolet. Daily we drove to the campus at 8 a.m. and spent the day there. This worked well until cold weather set in and the car refused to start. Walking to campus on frigid Minnesota winter days was agonizing.

When the cold walk became unbearable, we agreed to take turns getting up and starting the car to keep the engine warm. I was to warm it up at midnight, Roy at 3 a.m. and Dale at 6 a.m. Often, though, Roy didn't wake up and the car didn't start at 7:30 a.m.

Our apartment was nearly as cold as the car. The temperature rarely rose above 60. The landlord controlled the thermostat, so we complained to him. He promised to set it higher. If he did, we never noticed it. We wrapped ourselves in blankets as we spent the evenings studying.

As winter progressed we faced another problem. D's behavior began to concern Roy and me. He missed classes and began losing things. He seemed distraught and unable to focus. Roy and I awoke one minus ten degree morning to find D missing.

The winter weather was setting record lows, my Chev wouldn't start, final tests were beginning and D was gone. He left no note or any other clue as to his whereabouts. Although both Roy and I feared for him, we managed to develop a plan to accomplish what; we thought; needed to be done. The first action we took was the most difficult. We located a pay phone, and because I knew D's parents better than Roy did, I called them to tell them what had happened.

I choked up during the conversation but they were under control. They asked question after question trying to get as much helpful information as possible. Finally, they thanked us and hung up.

We walked the frigid two-mile journey to campus, occasionally escaping the wind by stepping into the doorways of stores or actually going into open restaurants. When we arrived on campus, we searched for D by monitoring his schedule. Because this required missing our own classes, we told our instructors what we were doing.

My Human Growth and Development professor, Dr. Murph Cansler, had asked each of his students to write their own final. While reading them, he would determine whether the student had learned the most important concepts taught in his class.

The assignment, which seemed difficult enough to begin with, now seemed overwhelming. Dr. Cansler, offered to ease my burden a bit, when he extended the deadline by two days.

After my visit with Dr. Cansler, we returned to the apartment hoping D had returned. He was not there. As we waited for him, we talked.

"He was telling us he was having problems and we didn't pay any attention," Roy said.

"When he lost his billfold and tore the house apart, I just kept on studying." I replied.

"I just thought he'd snap out of it."

"Where do you think he is?"

"I have no idea. I don't think he knows anyone around here."

This conversation repeated itself with no new ideas being offered other than deciding to attend finals the next day and to try as best we could to prepare for them in our remaining time.

After three days D arrived safely at his parent's home. He had hitchhiked the entire ninety miles. Lacking money to rent a room, he had slept in whatever shelter he found. He was physically fine but needed some time to recuperate from the recurring demons that plagued his early life.

My memory of the final exams that quarter and the relief that usually follows them, the break that follows that and the beginning of the next quarter have all faded or been lost to the anguish that followed what happened with D.

At the end of the 1960-1961 school year my funds were depleted, so I returned to work at the Foshay. In the fall I was able to reenroll. The National Defense Education Act had been enacted under President Eisenhower and I had been awarded seven hundred dollars to complete the 1961-62 school year. I hoped to finish school in the original four year time frame. For the first time since starting college, I was confident of graduating and I was finally looking forward to taking only classes in my major and minor that truly interested me.

Senior Year at last

The first problem to be solved was, as always, locating affordable housing. This year, though, I had several friends from Echo, who were attending college. The best news was that D had recovered and was ready to continue his education. D's younger brother, Dennis

Johnson, and Paul Tongen were now students at Mankato State and also wished to share an apartment with us. Roy had failed to report for his compulsory reserve requirement that followed his two years of active service in the military and had been redrafted.

The five of us found an apartment at 212 East Liberty Street, only three blocks from the campus. It was unfurnished but had a large kitchen, living room, bathroom, and one small bedroom. We located two bunk beds, and I slept on a small fold-up bed between them. For twenty-five dollars a month we lived in the lap of luxury.

As is with most college roommates there were some tense moments. Paul Tongen was a terrible tease, and Dennis Johnson was very sensitive. They were a bit like Abbott and Costello, Martin and Lewis or the Smothers Brothers. Tongen was vastly superior in physical strength and knew he could light Denny's fuse with no real danger of repercussions.

As the oldest member of our group I became the referee in their battles. One thing Tongen tormented Denny about was his family's wealth and income. Denny's mother taught school and his father farmed, so Paul would open the door to the ensuing battle by saying, "Denny doesn't need to work. He's from a two income family." Then he would begin to chant his mantra, "Two-income family, two-income family, two-income family." Dennis always responded and eventually prepared to take a swing at Tongen.

At that point I usually jumped between them shouting, "Knock it off!"

Tongen was considerably bigger and stronger than me but he usually laughed and said something like, "It's OK Denny, I wish I had a two income family too." Actually, his father farmed and his mother worked at a women's clothing store in Redwood Falls.

Paul's other sure fire routine to arouse Denny's ire was to grab Denny by both cheeks of his buttocks and say, "I can help you with your problems Denny. I've got Oral Roberts healing powers." Then, doing his best Oral Roberts imitation, he would shout, "HEAL! YOU ASSHOLE! HEAL!

One time Paul wasn't the villain. All of us, with good-humored intentions, played a practical joke on Denny. Registration for winter quarter opened at 8 a.m. Monday. Denny was obsessed with registering for a popular class and knew he would need to be in line at 7:00 a.m. or lose the opportunity. The weather was miserable with the temperature hovering below zero. He had his alarm set for 6 a.m. to give himself plenty of time. While I distracted him, D set the time on his alarm clock forward three hours. Denny rose at 3 a.m. and walked the three blocks to Old Main in the bitter cold. When he got there and recognized his error, he was livid. He exploded upon his return home, waking us all to lambaste us for our cruelty.

My roommates and I traveled together back home most weekends and were rewarded by our families with foodstuffs to sustain us for the following week. We brought back meat, cookies, buns and even milk from the farm. We took turns cooking and cleaning up our apartment and ate meals together. Evenings we studied. Our lifestyle was Spartan.

The rules at Mankato State on alcohol consumption and female companionship were clear and enforced. Underage students caught with alcohol in their rooms were suspended for one year. We feared that and complied. We never once had liquor in our apartment while I lived there.

Girls were not allowed to socialize with boys in their off-campus housing. That usually wasn't important because none of us were dating anyone. Once, however, three Echo girls visited us briefly to take a peek at our new digs. Betty Phillips, a business professor at the college, lived in an apartment below us and saw the girls arrive. That evening she left a note on our door warning us of the school code violation. These consequences were severe enough for us. Even when I was twenty-one years old and engaged to be married, there were no more code violations.

I planned carefully and found a path to graduation by August l962. I would earn a major in history and minors in English and geography and complete my student teaching during spring quarter. There was no room for error. Failing or dropping a class would upend the plan. I had never dropped or failed in the past and was confident I wouldn't in the future. The only difficulty I might encounter was Dr. Bill Lass. He was rumored to be a bit of a tyrant and my plan included successful completion of two of his Minnesota history classes. I registered for the first fall quarter.

I got a surprise when Dr. Lass entered the classroom on the first day. He was a diminutive, early middle-aged man, wearing dark pants, and a long-sleeved white shirt. He moved quickly to the front in silence before glancing at the class, pausing, saying nothing, unbuttoning his sleeves and rolling them up to the elbow. He then proceeded to review his class syllabus aloud in a soft, monotone voice. He seemed more of a bore than a tyrant.

As the quarter wore on, his routine didn't change but my appraisal of him did. His knowledge of the coming of age of the railroads, the role of wheat in the state's early development, the names and roles of all the players in Indian affairs in Minnesota and the route Minnesota took to statehood was impressive.

During examinations he seemingly revealed a Napoleonic complex. He rearranged the room by moving the desks apart and continually paced the aisles, occasionally stopping to read partial responses on student's papers. He made us aware that any form of cheating violated his ethical standards and would be treated with both expulsion from the class and a failing grade.

To achieve my required credits for graduation, I took a course in Canadian history. There were no history classes that were very appealing. With no better choices available the credits still counted toward my major.

Although the knowledge I acquired in the class proved to be minimal, the decision to take it was the most important decision of my college life.

When I entered the classroom the first time, I was surprised by the small number of students. Of the 15 or so students in the room, one captured my attention immediately. She was petite and eye-catching.

Everything about her was perfect. The sparkle in her eyes as I sat down by her, followed by her warm greeting and the ease with which our conversation flowed made me immediately comfortable.

At the end of the period I walked her down the stairs to the lobby and elicited the vital information, shooting questions at her faster than a cop interrogating a suspect. I had learned her name was Sheryl Preston so I started with determining her residence.

"Where are you from?' I demanded.

"Mankato," she replied.

"Where in Mankato?"

"On the upper west side—223 West 8th Street."

"Do you live with a bunch of girls?"

"No, I live with my mom. She's a teacher here in Mankato."

"I suppose you're dating someone and I don't have a chance."

"No I just broke up with a guy," she laughingly replied.

Then she said, "I've got to catch the bus home. I'll see you tomorrow in class."

My feet didn't touch the ground as I walked alone to Liberty Street. The next day after history class, I was more prepared. I had rehearsed our conversation in my mind to be certain it would be effective.

Before class I was cool. I began the conversation with Dr. Allen and Canadian history, but when class ended I sprung like a fox after a chicken. "Would you like to go to a movie this Friday?" I asked.

"Sure," she said. "I work at the theater so I have a free pass for two to all the movies in town. The tickets will be on me."

Wow! I thought. *I have found the right girl.* I considered asking her if she also got free popcorn but decided that might be pushing it.

Fortunately, I was able to provide us with the transportation for our date. Tongen, the Redetzke boys and I had purchased a 1948 Plymouth sedan for $50.00. We had each kicked in $12.50 and saved money by not transferring or insuring the car. To support homecoming queen candidate, Sharon Oakland, we had painted white stripes on our black sedan and used the slogan; "Oakland will skunk the other candidates." On campus the car had become known as the skunk.

This was the vehicle I used for my first date with Sheryl. From that day forward, unless Sheryl or I was working, we were together.

We studied together, ate together and went to movies—lots of movies. We usually did have enough money to pay for popcorn.

I met Sheryl's mother, Lucile, for the first time when I was invited to dinner. She prepared pork chops with mushroom gravy, mashed potatoes and string beans. Starting to eat my pork chop, I cut two pieces.

Lucile, in her best teacher's voice, said, "Emily Post, in her book on etiquette, recommends to cut only one piece of meat and eating it before cutting the second piece."

74

"Thanks for telling me that," I stammered. Inside though, I was upset and uncomfortable in her presence.

On December 1st I purchased an engagement ring from Goodman's Jewelry in downtown Mankato for $140. I put $40.00 down and asked for credit for the remaining $100.

On December 7, 1962, I walked Sheryl to the bus stop after class, handed her the diamond ring, and asked her to marry me. I was confident she would accept because we had already discussed marriage plans but her enthusiastic response was gratifying.

"I don't want to go home now," she said. "Let's take a walk."

The walk downtown was exhilarating but chilly. To warm up we stepped into the Red Owl store on the corner of Broad and Main. The first person we met was Dr. Cyril Allen. Sheryl held her ring finger out to him and said, "You're partially responsible for this. We met in your class."

We knew he was aware of the budding romance because he occasionally teased us with little comments like, "Mr. Stoufer and Miss Preston—would it be all right with you if I dismissed class a bit early today?" Now he looked at the ring and said, "Good job, Mr. Stoufer."

Although I have never believed I deserved it, both Sheryl and I were awarded an "A" in Canadian history.

Our new grade slips showed our standing in the class and I had moved to the top fourth. The only major hurdle left in my struggle to earn a college degree was student teaching. I had been placed at Central Junior High in Albert Lea and Sheryl had been placed in the senior high school in Waseca. We were excited and apprehensive about the coming experience.

My supervising professor Dr. James was unimpressive. He offered little instruction. I did not tell him of the obstacle I faced in my placement. I had no car. My only mode of transportation was hitchhiking. A solution to that appeared when Sheryl and I spent a weekend in Echo with my parents.

Even though the clientele and ownership had changed since I had left Echo four years ago, nostalgia always drove me to frequent the pool hall. One Saturday afternoon during Christmas break I was surprised when I walked in and immediately spotted my old buddy, Gene Kissner. Instead of indulging ourselves in a game of "Buck," we swapped stories and caught up on where life had us at the moment.

Gene had already met Sheryl and had immediately taken to her. He was delighted when I told him we were engaged.

"Henry," he said. "I told you before to hang onto this one. I'm glad you took my advice. She's a pistol."

"I guess I got lucky. Now I've got to get through this damned student teaching. I've always been on the other side of the teacher's desk. I'm not certain if the teacher's chair will fit me as well as the student's did."

"You'll be fine. If you don't like it, you got the degree and you can do something else. What the hell! You can dig graves or move corpses like you did in high school."

"I hope those days are over. The first problem I need to solve, if I'm going to teach in Albert Lea, is transportation. I don't have a car that runs. I won't even be able to get to the school."

"What do you mean you don't have a car?"

"We sold the old Plymouth."

Gene thought for a second and said, "You can have mine. I don't need it. I took a leave from Honeywell and enlisted in the Army. For the next two years they're going to provide me with transportation."

"Your car is almost new. I can't afford that. I don't get paid for student teaching."

"I'm not worried about that. Pay me when you start making some money. I won't need money in the Army."

Gene's car was a blue, two door 1960 Chevrolet Bel-Aire hardtop. It was beautiful. I carried collision insurance but not liability. If I smashed the car, I wanted to take care of my buddy but couldn't afford to protect the victim.

My assignment was teaching seventh-grade English and social studies with Mrs. Ives as my supervisor. Outside of a pretty decent knowledge of American history, I was totally unprepared. I knew nothing about classroom management, clerical responsibilities, or English grammar.

Mrs. Ives helped me prepare the first few lessons and stayed with me for a week. Then I was on my own. Most of the kids in my class were good and one was amazing. She taught me far more than I taught her.

Linda Marzinske had been born with birth defects that would have been completely disabling for many other people. Her left arm ended at the elbow and her right arm extended to her wrist but ended in a one-fingered hand. One leg seemed a bit longer than the other but both were short. Linda wrote beautifully, wrapping her good finger around her pencil. While not all of her papers were perfect, her work was always done promptly and satisfactorily. She received few special accommodations from the school, despite the fact that Central was a decrepit old building. The floors had buckled in many places, the windows leaked, the heat was inconsistent and the stairwells were narrow and crowded. It was an uninviting atmosphere for a disabled child but Linda thrived.

Other students like Georgia Boettcher, were also impressive. She sought more learning opportunities rather than less. When her assignments were finished she asked for more to do.

Richard was another story. As I was giving an assignment or discussing a lesson, he would walk to the window and look outside.

"Richard! I would say. "Take your seat."

"No," came the calm response. "I want to look outside."

This dumbfounded me. I expected prompt compliance and an apology.

When I reviewed my failure to adequately deal with the problem Mrs. Ives said only, "Yes, Richard can be difficult." Not much help in resolving the situation there.

The one time that Dr. James observed me, he offered even less guidance. He suggested, "Ask him what's so interesting outside?" Maybe you'll develop a better relationship with him."

I didn't want a warmer relationship with Richard. I wanted his respect.

As the quarter progressed, most students responded well to my leadership and I became more at ease and less threatened by challenges like Richard's. I spent evenings correcting papers, preparing lessons, and planning responses to problems that might arise.

On Friday evenings I drove to Waseca and picked up Sheryl and we usually visited my parents in Echo. Weather permitting, I set tombstones with Dad on Saturdays to earn cash to support myself the following week.

Over Easter weekend, while visiting Mom and Dad, I received a telephone call from Sherwood Clausen, the superintendent of the school in Stewart. Although I had not completed my student teaching experience, I had begun seeking employment as a teacher for the following year. I had left my parents telephone number on file and he called them to arrange an interview with me for a teaching position. Ready or not, this was the real deal.

When I was interviewed on Easter Monday, I was offered a position teaching two sections of English 9, two sections of American History 10 and supervising a study hall.

I knew I was poorly prepared to teach English. My English minor consisted of 24 credits. I had taken two introductory three-credit composition courses and no grammar classes. Despite my fears I accepted the position.

Sheryl and I had set our wedding date for August 25th. So when she was offered a teaching position in nearby Brownton, she accepted their offer to be their senior high English teacher. We rented a modest house in Stewart for $40 a month and prepared for our new life. Although Sheryl received A's and I earned B's for the student teaching experience, the grades were rather meaningless as we were *moving on up*.

What I Learned and What I Didn't

At the end of my undergraduate study, I left college to teach English. I was only slightly better prepared than when I graduated from high school. Thanks to assistant professor, Vern Winter, I had a decent grasp on Shakespearean literature and having completed a random selection of courses in American literature, I appreciated Frost, Sandburg, and Dickinson.

I had not studied Cooper, Irving, Twain, Whitman, Hemingway, Fitzgerald, Steinbeck, Faulkner, or any of the more contemporary American writers. The chasm in my knowledge of American literature was as deep as the Grand Canyon and as wide as the Atlantic Ocean.

I was even less prepared to teach English literature. I had taken only two survey courses that had included a smattering of Chaucer and Donne and a bit of Browning, James, and Conrad. The two Shakespeare classes I took were inspiring. I became familiar with his wordplay and character development and enjoyed digging my way through the riddles that abounded in his writing.

The only composition classes that were required were the freshman survey courses. In the first course we wrote one composition a week. We read from a variety of sources and chose our topic from one of them. The compositions were corrected, graded, and handed back with no opportunity available to benefit further from the written comments on them.

The second course required writing a research paper. Evelyn Hunt taught the basics of research by following a regimen that forced us to use the tools of research. From selecting the topic to proper documentation she walked us through the rudiments of research and held us accountable when we completed our papers.

When I completed her class I knew how to write a research paper. The content and documentation on my paper were acceptable but I had never taken a grammar course and it showed.

My major prepared me to teach American and European political history but was weak on cultural study. Beyond examining the role of the Japanese and the Chinese in wars, little study was required about Asia. The European history classes taught by Dr. Moir were demanding and prepared me to outline the political history of Europe. Drs. Allen and Lass offered the same level of instruction in American history.

Although I was not a historian by any means, I felt qualified to teach European and American history when I graduated from college.

The education courses I took did little to help me be a more effective teacher. They lacked focus and a coherent curriculum. The only class that gave practice in teaching was an English methods class from Professor Maakestad. He required us to teach a mini-lesson and then critiqued it.

Student teaching was a powerful learning experience but my college professor, Dr. James, made no contribution to it. It was sink-or-swim. A successful learning environment required carefully planned and executed lessons. Managing students also took planning and execution. Those things weren't taught at college but were learned from experience.

MIMEOGRAPH ERA

Stewart High School, Stewart, MN 1962-1965

Learning to be a Teacher

Work and fun were tied together
in my teaching life.
I did my best to keep that true.
It caused me much less strife.

Life, like race cars in the Indy 500, often makes sharp turns at high speeds. From August 22, until August 29th my life careened so rapidly that any efforts to apply the brakes, had little effect. On August 22 I graduated with my bachelor of science degree with a major in history and minors in English and geography. On the 25th Sheryl LaRita June Preston and I were married at Centenary United Methodist Church in Mankato. On the 29th, I attended my first day of workshop as a teacher in the Stewart Public Schools. My stress level was at a record high. It seemed to my family, especially my new wife, Sheryl, I had little confidence in succeeding in any of these new endeavors. I sometimes expressed a desire to return to the simpler life I had known as a child in Echo. Sheryl bore with me and supported me as I adjusted to the new circumstances.

Three years later, having completed a successful probationary teaching period, I served with fellow teachers, Merv Elwood, and Val Whipple on the first salary negotiating team in Stewart's school history. During a negotiating session, board chairman Klammer, a wealthy mink farmer, clarified his position on our status as teachers when he told us "we consider ourselves a teacher training ground, and we consider you fellows trained."

I had survived and even enjoyed my three years teaching in Stewart but still knew Klammer was wrong. I needed to grow a great deal more before I could call myself a fully trained teacher. That growth would require experience and formal training. His declaration, however, forced me to review what I had already learned about myself as a teacher and the requirements of my profession in Stewart.

I knew by now that teaching 30 students in a classroom with varying interests and abilities was far more complex than his simplistic view implied. When I had signed my contract with the school board in 1962, I had accepted the responsibilities to teach Stewart's children. I hoped to provide them with the skills to find truth in news filled with distortions; to organize their writing so that the message was meaningful and comprehensible; to enjoy finding contemporary applications in classical literature; to recognize the role of historic precedent in our contemporary world; and to experience the fulfillment from growing in knowledge. I knew I had not accomplished all of those goals. I had a long way to go.

Although I still considered myself a novice I was certain my training would continue in a different setting. After three years of minimal salary increases, I had become too expensive for Stewart. That spring, accepting that fact, I signed a contract to teach American History and English at Lincoln Junior High School in Mankato.

Before I accepted the Mankato job I reviewed my experience in Stewart and felt confidence that I would succeed.

The opening day of workshop my first year in Stewart, I had searched for textbooks for the two sections of English nine that I was to teach. I quickly located the Warriner's English Grammar but couldn't find the literature texts. Since I had graduated from college with a weak minor in English, not knowing a verb from a noun, I was convinced that if I was expected to successfully teach English, I desperately needed those literature texts. They were to be my primary source for imparting wisdom to my students.

When I accepted the position in Stewart, the principal had assigned me two sections of English 9 and promised to assist me with any concerns I might have. I immediately sought him out to help me find the literature texts. His response was swift and established the foundation for our future relationship. "Oh yeah, if we have any lit books, they're probably in the storeroom by the office. I suggest you look there."

I searched the building digging through every cabinet in every classroom, but came up empty handed. The help I needed came in the form of my wife. At the stage of marriage when most new brides were still honeymooning, English major, Sheryl, was tutoring me on the eight parts of speech. As I completed the exercises in the Warriner's grammar text, Sheryl corrected them.

New teachers in 1962 were expected to solve problems on their own. They learned to swim in the swift current of teaching or drown. To avoid drowning, I quickly learned to inventory materials well in advance of the school year.

That first year I promptly sought, and thankfully was given, permission by the superintendent, Sherwood Clausen, to order the literature textbooks I desired. When they arrived I was able to mix the literature and grammar. During the first weeks of school I worked hard at mastering grammar. Later instead of experiencing panic, it was pleasant preparing the assignments and I became a decent teacher of it.

From my work in Stewart, I learned the simplest but most important lesson in staff development. Do it yourself by inventorying, examining, and understanding all of the materials you will be using well in advance of teaching from them.

I also learned in Stewart that having a strong knowledge of the curriculum does not preclude the need for careful daily preparation. My first year teaching I was typically little more than a day ahead of the students. If I had been busy the night before with something else, the next day's lesson suffered and I likely had problems teaching it. In ninth-grade English these problems were personified in the form of Sue, one of my students. She drove me absolutely nuts if I showed uncertainty while teaching grammar.

She was a plain girl whose parents had led her to believe she was the center of the universe. My distaste for her attitude sometimes showed. Sue was an important incentive for me to prepare carefully. I hated being corrected by her. She had transferred from the parochial school, where the nuns had drilled grammar daily. She was more prepared to teach grammar than I was. If I called an indirect object a direct object, she corrected me. If I paused while identifying a part of speech, she filled in the pause. Eventually, she began to bring difficult sentence constructions from her parochial school papers to stump me in front of the class.

Sheryl's teaching responsibilities engulfed her time and energy, leaving me on my own to prepare for Sue's onslaught. Desperate, I sought help from the 10th grade English instructor, Jerry Johnson. During our prep period I studied with an intensity far beyond what I had exercised while preparing for final exams in college. I left no stone unturned while getting ready for Sue's attack. It had become personal. When Sue learned she could no longer stump me, the joy in her game disappeared and she stopped playing it. Then it seemed her appearance changed and she became a cute, little kid. I warmed to her parents, too.

Later in my career the concept of peer coaching was formalized and I was often assigned to mentor new teachers in the district just as Jerry Johnson had mentored me in Stewart. Because of Jerry's mentoring and Sue's challenging I learned to prepare well every day and encouraged mentees to do the same.

Most of the students in Stewart didn't challenge their teachers. They were eager to please. Some prepared their lessons more carefully than others, but almost all were well mannered and pleasant. Some were even willing to provide leadership in class. Ron Kirchkoff was one of them. Once when I was detained on the way to class, Ron, an excellent student and the quarterback of the football team, had taken attendance and started the class when I arrived. He was continuing a lesson on the U.S. Constitution we had started the previous day. He read a section of the document and asked the follow-up questions. Other students were responding.

The study hall I monitored, though, set the bar for low performance. The students refused to study, made a mess of the room and were noisy. I was frustrated but uncertain what to do. I disliked confrontation and was unsure of the mores' for study hall behavior. My weak attempts to gain control included quietly correcting offending students.

For example, I might say, "Judy, It's important that you get your work done now" or "Tom, you're bothering Chris. Please let him work."

Other times I threatened the class with meaningless consequences like, "If you don't quiet down now, I'll send you to the principal!" Students knew this threat was meaningless as the principal was ineffective.

About the fourth week of school, Dean Klitzke, a mild-mannered, quiet student approached me and pleaded, "Please quiet this place down. I have to work after school, and I've got to finish my assignments here." I knew then that I must take charge and developed a plan.

That plan included the use of a yardstick as a prop. I held the yardstick in my hands and informed the students there would be changes in their study hall behavior. When Rollie, a 10th grader, turned around and started whispering, I slammed the yardstick down on his desk smashing it into a hundred pieces that flew in all directions. Rollie was the perfect target for this performance. He was a cocky, good-looking kid who always pushed the envelope. His dad operated the local café, where he hung out with all the kids in town. Silence fell over the room as I shouted, "Leave this room immediately, LaPlante, and don't come back until your parents are with you."

Rollie's mother called the office later that day and arranged a meeting with me. The word spread and study hall became more tolerable. I may not have chosen the best course of action but it was a step for me in learning the art of classroom management. It had become clear to me that it was necessary to provide an atmosphere where students could learn.

My colleague, Val Whipple was only 21 years old but was more adept at classroom management than I was. He was hired as the head basketball coach and 12th grade social studies teacher. At the end of the football season, most of the junior and senior boys who would have been basketball players were caught "celebrating" and weren't allowed to play basketball that year. "Whip" handled the investigation and assigned the consequences. The situation left our team young and inexperienced. Over the next two years we lost a long string of games. It seemed endless, but Whip understood the game better than I did and somewhere in the middle of his second season, he recognized that our players were becoming competitive. He expected them to win. I and many of the team members were less certain.

The Renville game was a breakthrough for us. We had beaten Cosmos already, but Renville, unlike Cosmos, was good. At halftime we were down by fifteen. I was ready to board the team on the bus and go home. Whip, though, saw opportunity, and gave the halftime speech of his life. I believed it was futile but he detailed how the game could be won. If we stepped up our offense and hustled back down court on defense we could win. He pointed at our 6-foot 5-inch center, Ted Burke, and shouted, "You've got to get back on defense faster. They're killing us with cheap baskets when you're not there to defend." Ted and the rest of the team followed his advice, took charge of the game and won in regulation time. Once again I was being trained—this time by a peer. Given encouragement and correct instruction kids will come through. Successful teachers challenge their students and expect winning results.

Good teaching also requires remembering that kids will be kids. Even though we were all children once, it is difficult to remember that a lack of experience can lead one to do dumb things. Teachers, as the adults, are responsible for recognizing that and responding appropriately. Sometimes I did, and sometimes I didn't.

I got it right with Jerry. He was not one of my students but was known all as a bit of a troublemaker. Three or four times while walking through the hall, he tried to bait me by looking me in the eye and calling me "Wally."

Another student told me he was referring to Wally Cox, an actor who played a bespectacled, nerdy high-school teacher who starred in a television series called, "Mr. Peepers." Both I and the other students paid no attention and the name calling ceased.

I didn't get it right with Kenny Goodman though.

One early spring day I was teaching my 10th grade U.S. History class when something hit one of the windows in our ground floor classroom. I hurried to the window and found no damage. Kenny Goodman, one of our senior boys, was moving hurriedly down the sidewalk.

I opened the window and shouted out, "Goodman, did you throw a stone at my window?"

"No!" He replied. "I threw a stone and it hit your window." Following his remarks he turned and continued to walk away from me. He kept walking.

Frustrated, I shouted. "Goodman, turn around and head for the principal's office. I'll meet you there."

He turned his head slightly and retorted, "I'm going home to work for my dad. I don't have time for this stupid stuff." With that he walked away leaving me frustrated and embarrassed. I turned to my class and said, "He won't get away with this."

Kenny had been my student when he was in 10th ,grade. I knew he resented being given directions. He was a six feet tall with an athletic build and a baby face. While not a bully, he was pushy and sometimes arrogant. The other kids liked him though, and he dated Eileen McGraw, one of the nicest girls in the school.

Between classes I hurried to the new principal and told him what had happened and requested appropriate and prompt consequences. I strengthened my case by recounting some of Kenny's past misbehaviors. The principal, Noel Pfieffer, told me later that he had denied Ken permission to go on the senior class trip to Chicago the following week.

Three years later, in 1968 I was teaching at Lincoln Junior High. During a prep period I was breezing through the *Minneapolis Tribune* when the name Ken Goodman caught my eye. The young Marine had been killed while trying to protect soldiers stationed near the Ho Chi Minh Trail. An unsent letter had been found among his belongings. In it he wrote to his parents of his deep love for them and for the country.

I thought a great deal about proportion that day and tried hard to be more judicious when administering discipline for the remainder of my career. As I gained experience I was more temperate in responding to situations like Kenny's. Overreacting did not build a solid classroom environment and its results sometimes proved destructive.

Effective modern schools promote collegiality among staff members. Good veteran teachers are rewarded for mentoring new, inexperienced teachers. This creates a strong support system and provides a safe place for novices to have their concerns acknowledged and deal with situations like the one I had with Ken. Veterans are able to identify serious problems from the routine or trivia of dealing with large numbers of children daily. They have the personal qualities that are necessary for long-term survival and success in the classroom. They are up to date on educational research and use best practices routinely in their classrooms. They are the best of the best in their classroom.

In 1962 in Stewart there were no formal mentoring programs for new teachers but there were mentors. Merv Elwood was a natural at it.

Merv had been teaching social studies and coaching basketball and football for seven years in Stewart. He and his wife, Fanch, a regular substitute teacher, were highly respected in the community and popular among students. Since I used different rooms to teach my classes, and Merv was a social studies teacher, he and I shared a classroom.

He quickly took me under his wing. I observed the casual, easy manner he displayed in his classroom and tried to emulate it. He was candid in his assessment of the troubling situation in Stewart's administration. "Our principal has a drinking problem. Just avoid him. He isn't helpful, but he isn't harmful either. If you have some concerns or questions, stop at our house. Fanch and I always welcome company. We have open house every night."

He was sincere. Although the Elwoods had three small children and were very busy, they always took the time to be helpful to new staff. They did it discreetly and warmly. They built trusting relationships. They preferred having people in their home to visiting others. That way they could maintain both a busy social life and a strong family life.

After homecoming they invited the whole staff, including Superintendent Clausen and his wife. There was a happy hour buffet with beer. The beer was supposed to be kept secret because schoolteachers were forbidden to drink alcohol.

Even though they were invited, nobody expected the Clausens to attend, because they rarely attended social events. When they did, anyone who had beer tried to hide it. That night I managed to slide my beer around the corner of a nearby bookcase. It was funny to watch the other guests hide their illicit beer.

The Elwood's support made my years in Stewart more productive and pleasant. I remain grateful for that to this day. Although we rarely see them we have shared Christmas letters for nearly fifty years. I know I was truly blessed to have these nurturers in my life as a beginning teacher.

"Whip" was single when we met at the Stewart teachers' workshop in 1962. He had graduated from high school in Ivanhoe, Minnesota and graduated from Gustavus Adolphus College with a major in history and physical education. The two of us became fast friends. We frequently swapped stories of our youth and commiserated about the challenges of teaching and coaching.

Whip often stopped in my room for a few minutes before school. He would greet me with, "What you doing today, Stouf? I wish I'd studied harder when I was in college." We'd both laugh, confident that we'd get through this first year and the job would get easier.

During the summer of 1963, our mutual friend, Merv Elwood, called one stormy afternoon and shared the sad news that Butch

Wacker, a talented, personable, local college kid was swathing peas for Green Giant when he was struck and killed by lightning.

Butch was a senior at St. Cloud State and about to accept his first teaching position. He had been an excellent athlete in high school and was managing the Stewart baseball team during the summer. His work ethic and dedication, had earned him the respect and admiration of the entire community. Through city baseball Whip and Butch had become close friends. Whip was asked to be a pallbearer at Butch's funeral.

Butch's sister Linn who had been teaching in Hawaii resigned her position there and came home to Minnesota. She accepted a teaching position as a girl's physical education instructor in Brownton, where Sheryl taught. When school started, they became friends. Because I was Whip's friend and Linn was Sheryl's, we arranged for the two of them to go out to dinner with us. That led to a whirlwind romance. They woke us at 4:00 a.m. a few months later to announce their plans to be married.

The Whipples moved to Minneota, and we moved to Mankato but the shared experiences of those early years of teaching forged a lifelong friendship. Friendships like this are among the most delectable of the fruits served up by the profession.

During the late summer of 1964 another old friend re-entered my life. I was spending some time in my classroom preparing for the beginning of the 1964-65 school, when much to my surprise my college roommate, D, entered the room with Superintendent Clausen. Clausen was smiling as he opened the conversation.

"Roger, I believe you know D. I've just hired him to be our fifth grade teacher."

I was so surprised I could have been "knocked off my chair with a feather." This was a great opportunity for us to renew our friendship. There had been several resignations over my two years in Stewart and our new staff, including D, contained seven males under the age of twenty-five.

D had completed the requirements for graduation and teacher certification at Mankato State and was excited about beginning his teaching career. He rented a room from a retired widow in the community and began work. Because I was working on my master's degree, I saw little of him during the weeks preceding school. I remembered my first year experience and empathized with him.

When school started, D seemed to lack focus. He came to my classroom expressing fear that he was incapable of doing the job. I noticed he was leaving his classroom frequently and wandering the halls. Late in the second week of school superintendent Clausen came to my room immediately after school. "Roger, you know D better than anyone here. I have genuine concerns about his behavior and am seeking your advice. I want to give him every chance to succeed. How might we assist him through this difficult time?"

"I know his parents well. They're good people. I think we should contact them."

Mr. Clausen paused. "I think it's best if we drive to Echo and visit with them directly. Are you free to do that?"

"Yes," I said. Sheryl and I had planned to go out to dinner but this easily took precedence. On the trip to Echo there were long quiet spells. Mr. Clausen was not a gambler but knew there was personal risk involved in trying to help D. If a problem arose while D was out of the classroom, he bore some responsibility. Yet he seemed driven to take that risk.

D's parents decided to drive back to Stewart behind us. I would take them them to D's house and they, along with D, would decide on a course of treatment. If D chose to continue to teach, Mr. Clausen would observe him closely.

D's landlady greeted us when we arrived and knocked on his door to announce our presence. He opened the door, took one look at me and said, "Stoufer, stay the hell out of my business. If I wanted your help, I'd ask."

I left immediately and walked the two blocks home. D's parents and I did not have any future correspondence about this. He returned to school on Monday and resumed teaching. I heard nothing else about his teaching or his behavior. He seemed to have a normal remainder to his first year teaching experience and we maintained our friendship.

Mr. Clausen was a diminutive, quiet, somewhat distant person. Occasionally he was referred to as weak, but I knew better.

D eventually married a strong, determined Stewart girl. He encouraged his new bride to attend Mankato State. She completed her degree in education and they both accepted teaching positions in another community where they raised their two children. They remained there until their retirement. Today their daughter is a doctor and their son a high school principal. Both are married and have families. My wife, Bev, and I remain good friends with the family.

Principals

"Tunee" was my first principal in Stewart. He was around fifty years old, about six feet tall, and enough overweight so his stomach pushed his shirt out, covering his view of his shoes. Every day he wore brown leather slippers, polyester jeans with a shiny seat, a multi colored Hawaiian shirt, and sunglasses. They hid the blindness in his left eye.

An unsteady gait forced him to lean against the lockers as he high stepped down the hallway between classes. Students sometimes followed mimicking him but he never reacted and neither did the staff.

Tunee was pleasant but not collegial. He hid in his office most of the school day and slipped unnoticed in and out of the building. The competence of the veteran teachers kept the school running smoothly. Tunee allowed himself minimal interactions, but uncharacteristically he occasionally reached out to a staff member. The most memorable of these attempts at bonding happened when he called Carsten Bjornson, the new tenth grade English teacher. The telephone conversation began, "Carsten, do you and your wife like fish?" Without waiting for an answer he went on. "I have a couple of nice bass that you can have. I'll be waiting for you to come get them."

The Bjornsons and Tunee's families lived in trailers on rented land less than a block from the school. Wanting to be polite, Carsten slipped on his jacket and walked the short distance.

When Tunee met him at the door, he was more disheveled than usual and slurred his words. "Don't bother to take your shoes off," he said as he picked up a pail half full of water that was sitting in the middle of the floor. "Follow me."

Carsten shadowed him to the bathroom, wondering where the rest of the family was and started to worry about their welfare. His focus shifted quickly when Tunee stopped at the bathroom door and motioned Carsten to follow him in. To his shock two bass were swimming in the tub full of water. "Oh, my God!" he exclaimed.

Tunee, ignoring him, kneeled down, pulled the drain stopper out and began thrashing his hands around in the water trying to capture the elusive bass. Carsten, stunned, stood motionless until Tunee shouted, "Get down here beside me! I need some help." In a matter of minutes, Carsten was carrying the pail of fish to his home. He now had the best of the multitude of *tails* that floated around the community about the high school principal.

Not long after that, Tunee left school one day and parked in the alley behind the liquor store in neighboring Buffalo Lake. Eventually he left, sliding through a stop sign and cutting into a funeral procession behind the hearse but in front of the deceased's son, who happened to be the chairman of the Stewart School Board. The next week Tunee was gone.

Over the years I have developed more sympathy for my first principal—a fundamentally decent and intelligent man. In the 1960's alcoholism was considered more a weakness than a disease.

Noel Pfieffer

Noel Pfieffer replaced Tunee and the contrast could not have been greater. Noel was 6' 1" and had an athletic build, and a purposeful walk. He dressed well and had a strong presence both in the school and the community. On his first day on the job, he met with students and staff and detailed how the school would function under his leadership. "The floors will shine, the bathrooms will be free of inappropriate graffiti, teachers and students will be courteous and prompt," he announced. "Taxpayers spend their money to provide a place for you to learn and that is what you will do here." He issued commands, not requests. Everyone in the auditorium knew it was the beginning of a new era.

"Fife" kept his promise. He was in the halls between classes monitoring student behavior and he inspected the bathrooms hourly for graffiti. He was an ever-present force in the lunchroom. He observed teachers in their classrooms. He attended events and was a vocal cheerleader for all activities, and he met with staff after work hours and sought their input.

The new agriculture teacher was having a difficult start-up year. Whenever Fife wasn't in the room the classroom became chaotic. The students were out of control and he didn't seem to notice. They threw paper airplanes, flipped pennies and stood atop their desks and still he lectured. Either he was able to utterly disregard the chaos or he was unable even to see it. Floyd kept lecturing.

Fife set up a staff development program for him. Two or three of us were assigned to mentor him. He was told to observe our classrooms. After observing a rare "perfect" hour in my room he said, "I can't see much difference in their behavior here and in my room."

I knew then that he was in big trouble. I left Stewart the next year and I think he did too.

Fife stayed a few years in Stewart before moving to Glencoe, where he was the junior high school principal until his retirement. I worked with a variety of principals after that, but none measured up to him.

Sheryl's First Principal

Sheryl was among the best teaching candidates of the 1962 graduating class candidates at Mankato State. While we were student teaching we decided that I would accept a teaching position first and Sheryl would seek one nearby. We wanted to have children as soon as possible after we were married. I would continue to work while Sheryl stayed home with the children. If my first job went well we might wait before moving on to a larger community.

Sheryl informed the college and The Rex Hill Placement Bureau in Mankato of her preference for a location near Stewart. We waited and waited anxiously because we were counting on two incomes

101

for the first year or two. Finally, the Bureau called and arranged an interview for Sheryl in Brownton. The new superintendent looked at Sheryl's credentials and offered her the job. He knew she was a catch.

She was to teach English 10, 11, and 12, direct the class play, and assist with speech activities—exactly what she wanted. She was confident and looked forward to proving herself.

The Principal was also a newcomer. When Sheryl came home after school she announced, "It's impossible to find the 'Super' when you need him and it doesn't do much good if you find the Principal. He refuses to hold students accountable."

As the year progressed she complained of the administrators less and spoke fondly of her students. She seemed comfortable with classroom management and enjoyed sharing her in depth understanding of the curriculum.

The second year was more difficult. One of the senior boys, was rude to her, refused to complete assignments and held court with his friends in class. When she finally removed him from class and asked him to make up the time after school, he didn't show up. When she asked him for make-up for his absences, he laughed. When she threatened to have him removed from class, he replied, "You don't have the authority to do that."

Sheryl met with her principal several times to discuss the problem. His advice usually went something like, "Rod has a bad temper. You'll need to lower your voice when you talk to him. That high pitched tone annoys him." Sheryl was expected to change rather than the student. She began to worry about her future ability to find a job.

Contracts were to be distributed to teachers by March 1st. Teachers who weren't receiving a contract were to be notified of their termination by then. The Brownton contracts were being placed in teacher's school mailboxes beginning in early February. Sheryl was curious about the uneven distribution but didn't become concerned until middle March during the state high school basketball tournament.

The Stewart school district was frugal with extra benefits for staff with the notable exception of state tournament bonuses given to the head and assistant basketball coaches. The district provided a three day hiatus for them. Mileage, hotel, meals and tournament tickets were all paid for.

Sheryl, and Whip's girlfriend, Linn, attended the Friday evening and Saturday games with us. When they arrived, I could tell something was wrong with Sheryl. Uncharacteristically, she appeared sad and uncomfortable. Within minutes she whispered to me, "I need to see you alone."

We excused ourselves and Sheryl shared with me, "I am not being given a contract to teach in Brownton next year. I asked the Super, "When am I getting my contract?"

He said, "You're not getting one." and I left the room in tears.

"They can't do that!" I said uncertainly. "There are laws about contracts. They've violated every one of them. We'll deal with this when we get home."

Sunday, we made a plan. Following the rule of law, we would force them to offer Sheryl a contract. She would not accept the contract and would seek employment in another community.

I arranged to meet with both administrators during Easter vacation. Sheryl did not want to be there. When I got to the office, only the principal was present. He quickly sought to intimidate me by saying, "This is a done deal. We have done what we are going to do and there are no alternatives."

My knees shook as I argued. The following discussion made little headway and I could sense he was gettting angry. His voice grew louder and his hand motions included a clenched fist. Staring at me he said, "I have a terrible temper. When I was coaching basketball in North Dakota, I grabbed a referee around the neck and had to be pulled off him."

"That would be very costly for you, if it happened today," I said.

After a long pause he replied "I'll talk to the Superintendent and see if we can get this thing done."

The next week Sheryl returned the unsigned contract she had been given by Superintendent with a letter of resignation. That summer she accepted a job in Hector, Minnesota and enjoyed working under their principal, Don Espenson.

What Worked and What Didn't

Even though I was better trained to teach history than English, I soon learned English, was easier for me to teach. After I explained the difference between direct and indirect objects students completed practice exercises. They became involved in the lesson and most tried hard to complete it.

In history classes I assigned readings and we discussed them. I tried to use the Socratic method but my students hadn't heard of Socrates and I lacked his intellect. After fifteen minutes the students were restless. I required them to answer assigned study questions on reading assignments but most of their responses were weak. I assigned research papers, but in spite of my warnings, most of the students thought plagiarized paragraphs from encyclopedias qualified as research. Eventually I assigned each student a portion of a topic to explain. One might be responsible to explain the Second Amendment while another might explain the role of James Madison in writing the constitution. I prepared myself to fill in the blanks. This format proved to be more effective.

I kept the tone casual and the students responded to it. I told jokes occasionally and visited with students about their activities and families. I wasn't much of a shouter, so I tried to reason with them but always held them accountable.

Primarily, though, I learned that teaching was hard work and required from me the discipline of grading papers and preparing lessons nightly. I also learned that a competent staff could run a school in spite of an incompetent principal. It became obvious that the real work took place in the classroom.

Most importantly, though, I learned that I could manage a classroom with 30 students and still help them learn.

What I didn't learn much about was diversity. The town of 700 citizens was approximately fifty-seven percent Lutheran, thirty-seven-percent Catholic, two percent Methodist and four percent mavericks.

The Catholics did an end run around the Lutheran school boards while I was there and by secrecy and stealth, managed to elect Dick Richards as a write in candidate. He proved to be an exceptionally good board member.

Nor did I learn much about conflict resolution. Each day was like the other one. I went to work free of the serious anxiety that plagues many schools.

At one point during my first year in Stewart I considered leaving the teaching profession. After three years there I was convinced I would remain a teacher the rest of my life.

Memorable Students

Ted Burke

Ted Burke, an athletic and handsome 6-foot 5-inch freshman in my ninth grade English class was a gentle soul and one of my most memorable students. He had a curious mind and read widely about issues like the probability of intelligent life beyond the planet earth. The Bermuda triangle was a popular topic for conversation in the early sixties, and Ted was well prepared to hold court. He often sat by me in a study hall I supervised and tried to to goad me into talking about it, knowing I doubted the existence of intelligent life elsewhere in the solar system.

Ted's talents created high hopes that he would lead Stewart to conference championships in basketball and football but his analytical mind led him to think things through rather than be reactive, but he progressed steadily and was awarded a football scholarship at the University of Minnesota where he became a starting center. He graduated with a degree in dentistry where I have heard he has regularly performed pro bono dentistry work for the needy. That is not surprising.

Peter Kasal

Peter Kasal and his identical twin Paul were both outstanding kids. Peter excelled in my American history class. On the standardized test that was given every spring measuring the depth of knowledge of the students, Peter scored in the 99th percentile. After law school he returned to McLeod County to become the county attorney. He has now returned to private practice and appears to be quite successful.

The Grabow Boys

The Grabow brothers, Jim, Bob and Dean were friendly boys and I enjoyed having them in class. So I was surprised, when, through careful investigation, I discovered they had soaped my windows on Halloween.

I spent some time pondering a course of action before calling Jim to my room to interrogate him. As he walked in I said, "Jim, why did you and your brothers soap my windows on Halloween night?"

Unhesitatingly he replied, "I'm sorry. We didn't plan to do it. We were walking by and Bob suggested it. We went home and got some soap. I didn't want to do it."

"Jim, Sunday I had planned to rake my lawn and had to clean my windows instead. Do you think you, Dean and Bob could help me rake my lawn next Saturday?"

"Sure," he said. "I'll tell them."

The next Saturday morning the Grabow boys and I raked the lawn together and Sheryl prepared lunch for us when we finished.

Laverna Redman

Laverna was in my first hour American history class my first year in Stewart. She was a bright kid and enjoyed challenging my interpretations of historical events. I sensed she wasn't trying to intimidate me but rather enjoyed the challenge I represented in debating her ideas. I, too, began to enjoy the verbal repartee. Although other students originally seemed bored, some eventually chimed in and challenged both of us. I sometimes sensed that other students in the class lost interest in our "coffee talk." But, I also discovered that other students enjoyed challenging Laverna's ideas and she loved the challenge.

Laverna taught me to use a student's strong personality as an effective teaching tool—a skill that came in handy for the rest of my career.

Epilogue

Stewart was the perfect site to begin my education career. It was welcoming, the students were well mannered, and the staff was encouraging. It was comfortable and I could easily have spent my entire teaching career there.

A Tale of a Teacher

OVERHEAD ERA

Lincoln Jr. High, Mankato, MN 1965-1977

Intermediate Teacher Training

I'm more prepared to do the job
this second time around.
The challenges seem greater though
the range of skills abounds.

My job and life in Stewart were nearly perfect. Although teachers couldn't spend time in the pool hall as I had as a kid in Echo, our crowd hobnobbed together at the social events in the community. Most of them took place in the school. Sporting events, class plays, concerts, and proms were part of the job. State tournaments, Gopher and Twins games, and professional theater were less than an hour away in the Twin Cities.

One evening was spent with the Whipples dining out in Hutchinson and the next with the Hofteizers seeing Cleopatra in downtown Minneapolis. When we weren't correcting papers or preparing lessons, we could often be found in the gym shooting buckets, where our single buddies Quentin Lundberg and Dale Redetzke might join us.

Just as anxiety and loneliness had set in when I left Echo, they returned when we left Stewart. But now, in Mankato for the second time, there were new joys and responsibilities. Our daughter Michelle was born March 11, and in June we moved into a small rented duplex on Grant Avenue in North Mankato. Due to her type 1 diabetes, Sheryl had lived in Mankato with her mother the last two months of her pregnancy. All had gone well, and both Sheryl and Shelly were fine. Now, living in Mankato, we had permanently secured quick access to meet our health concerns.

We had two major concerns at that time. One was financial. We had lived well on two incomes but now planned to survive only on my annual gross income of $5,800. Our rent and utilities budget was $2,000, leaving little for luxury. Our new life looked like all work and no play. Our second, more critical concern was the Viet Nam War. The United States was becoming more involved and society was unsettled.

Despite that, we looked forward to meeting the staff and developing new friendships in Mankato but that had to wait until workshop in August. To prepare for school, I spent many days working at Lincoln but didn't feel very welcome. The custodians were preparing the building for opening day and were inhospitable.

At my first workshop session with the Lincoln staff, I was disappointed to find that nearly all the staff members were considerably older. When the session broke for lunch, no one invited me to eat with them. I drove home alone and had a sandwich with Sheryl. This was nothing like Stewart.

At the end of the three day workshop, the environment hadn't warmed. It was clear that until I proved myself, I would be considered an outsider. I could live with that. Unlike in Stewart, my social life would now be separate from my work life.

I had learned a great deal in Stewart. There would be no more lost literature books or ignorance of the curriculum. My course outline for the school year was finished, the first week's lesson plans were complete to the last detail, with a content that would challenge even the brightest students, and the classroom environment was warm with applicable colorful bulletin boards in place. I had done my best.

The pieces that weren't in place quickly became evident when the year began. The next part of my training would take place at Lincoln Junior High in Mankato, Minnesota.

The district had hired Dr. Jack Sjostrom as curriculum director. His early role was to draft and publish sequential curriculum guides for all the disciplines taught. They were to cover every concept taught and to establish the appropriate level of student understanding of each. Verbs, for example, were taught simply in seventh grade, complexly in ninth grade and everything was reviewed in tenth and eleventh.

Dr. Sjostrom supervised as the teachers worked to outline the scope and sequence of language skills for 7th through twelfth grade skills. Even though it was my first year in the district, I was chosen to write the 7th grade English portion.

The English curriculum writers met to decide what would be taught and which resources to use in presenting them. Irony was taught simply in seventh grade using O Henry's *Ransom of Red Chief*. Teachers were encouraged to use secondary sources to expand on the lesson.

These guides proved to be effective tools for all teachers but they were especially helpful for teachers new to the district.

Learning to Accommodate Students Different Learning Styles and Speeds

During my first year at Lincoln I was assigned four sections of English 7 and one section of 7th grade U.S. History. The average class size was twenty-eight students, larger than at Stewart. Reading comprehension skills varied from 3rd to 12th grade. Not trusting the scores on the Iowa Basic Skills tests, I held private reading sessions with students to help determine each student's reading level. The picture that emerged was complex. While preparing for classes I was aware of the differing needs and struggled to accommodate them.

My Classes included Steven Duane, a budding oncologist; Kim Schwickert, a future CEO; Steve Plocher, a soon-to-be naval cadet and Sally Thompson, who was already preparing to be a technical writer. Ben, Rose, Peter and John couldn't read. It was my job to help each student reach their maximum capability. I felt I was climbing that ladder barefoot.

By now, a proficient grammar teacher, and firm in the belief that students needed to learn to write proficiently, I started the year teaching the eight parts of speech. Duane, Schwickert, Thompson and Plocher whizzed through their assignments. Ben, Rose, Peter, and John found it impossible to understand them. It was hard work developing ways to help them grasp the concepts and times for tutoring. I made myself available both before and after school. Transportation was an obstacle before school and schedules made meetings difficult after school and many who were tutored continued to struggle.

John, a warm, articulate kid arranged to meet with me during my preparation period three hours a week for help with grammar. He attended every session for several weeks. He was attentive and polite but the light never came on for him. He seemed unable to master the requirements. I was stumped. My mind searched for ideas to solve the problems all the Johns were having in mastering the grammar curriculum. I arranged a meeting with Dr. Sjostrom to discuss grouping students according to their ability.

His response was swift and firm. "That's not going to happen, Roger. All the research clearly informs us that ability grouping results in loss of self-esteem and creates lower levels of learning."

Wally McDougal, the new math teacher had been assigned five sections of ninth-grade general math, more commonly known as bonehead math. He taught classes that had been grouped by ability.

Many of his students were defiant and difficult to manage. His frustration spilled out every time we talked. My situation, although imperfect, seemed better than his.

Problems like these were accepted at Lincoln and teachers worked on their own to solve them. The district, struggling with minimal resources, offered no relevant staff development. Teachers were encouraged through salary schedule rewards to continue their education in graduate school, but little monitoring was done to determine whether that helped their students learn in the classroom.

Visiting in the lounge, we shared our experiments in trying to overcome the obstacles of learning. Ron Hibbard, the ninth grade algebra teacher, was grouping students, to encourage those who were more advanced to help those who were struggling. That seemed like it had potential. It seemed logical that a flyer might be able to help a crawler to a faster pace. However, both groups were uncomfortable with it.

Another approach was differentiated assignments. Better students were given A assignments while others were given B assignments in the same class. Both taught the same concepts but the B assignments were given simpler constructions. This required increased preparation time and stronger organizational skills.

Over time, research resulted in other models for teachers to use, but none were completely successful. In 35 years of teaching I never mastered individualized instruction. I was still working on it when I retired. The coaches were the most skilled at individualizing instruction and often were among the best teachers.

The Teacher Benefits of
Extra-Curricular Assignments

I was a mediocre athlete in high school, but the things I learned about both football and basketball allowed me to coach at the junior high school level. Although not a master strategist, I understood the fundamentals of basketball and football and had some success in coaching them in Stewart. At Lincoln those coaching positions were filled and I became the head gymnastics coach. As a student, not only had I never been a gymnast, I had never even attended a gymnastics meet.

Eldon Peterson, the physical education instructor, was the first staff member to reach out and welcome me. He coached both eighth grade football and gymnastics. Early on he informed me he wanted me to help him in both sports. I reminded him repeatedly of my lack of my knowledge in gymnastics and he repeatedly assured me of his willingness to help me learn the basic routines. The five different components of gymnastics were floor exercise, pommel horse, parallel bars, high bar and trampoline. Each could be dangerous, but the trampoline was life threatening.

Coach Peterson worked with me just as he worked with the student athletes, and soon I understood the requirements of all the compulsory exercises in each event. I couldn't do any of them but I understood how they were done and learned to spot athletes to protect them from injury.

Fortunately our athletes were; for the most part, very disciplined. The combination of their work ethic and talent and Coach Peterson's leadership skills enabled us to be a very competitive team. We lost only one meet to Fairmont and we defeated them in our second meeting. The first year as assistant coach proved rewarding.

I wasn't, however, prepared for what happened next. At the end of the season "Pete" resigned as head coach and recommended me for the position. I vigorously objected but John J. Nelson, our principal, insisted. Like the former naval officer he was, he appointed me head coach.

Warren Mickelson, the geography teacher and a new friend, became my assistant. His qualifications were similar to mine. We were quite a pair. For practices we decided each of the gymnasts would be an all-around gymnast working every event. There were 40 gymnasts and five events. That meant eight gymnasts worked together and each team had a captain. This way we shared the responsibility of coaching with the kids and they stepped up to the plate. The leaders included Kim Schwickert, who eventually won the state championship in floor exercise; Steve Duane, who was his runner-up; Jim Nelson, who placed, and Steve Plocher, who placed in pommel horse.

Mick and I learned from the kids. We asked for coaching tips and sometimes even tried to perform. I proved to be a great example of what not to do, when, while attempting a flank vault dismount from the pommel horse, I broke my ankle.

Making the students assistants turned what might have been a disastrous season into a successful one. As I matured, this became a common practice in all my classes. Students who were more skilled than I helped other students advance and I grew by observing them.

The second year Mick and I coached together we encountered another difficult decision. Becky Paul excelled at floor exercise. Since the public schools offered no opportunities for girls to participate athletics, Becky had to participate at the YMCA and at summer camps. Her older brother, Eric, had been a superior gymnast at Mankato High School and in college. When Becky asked if she could practice with our boys we responded with a hearty, "Let's do it!"

Both of us were confident that we could manage the problems that might arise from our decision. A few days later, Orv Schwankl, the district athletic director, called. He shouted, "What in God's name are you guys doing?" Girls can't compete in boys sports. There are all kinds of legal issues that could arise. In addition to that, other schools won't want their boys competing against girls. What if she beats their boys?"

"She will," I replied. She's a better gymnast than most of our guys right now."

For about ten minutes, Orv continued to take chunks out of my derriere while I defended my position. Finally we agreed on a compromise, when he said, "If you take proper precautions, she can continue to practice with your team, but she cannot participate in meets.

Although this did not fully satisfy Becky, it was a small victory. The unfolding of equal opportunity for girls in high school and college sports unfolded slowly until 1972, when Title IX finally settled equality for girls into law.

Be careful—Don't buy into every new idea

In the late 1960's, while the rest of America was buzzing about manned space flight to the moon, English teachers in Mankato were engrossed in conversations about transformational grammar. To standardize and simplify grammar teaching some researchers had developed a binary system that used almost a mathematical approach to explain the language system.

Attempting to be on the cutting edge of the new model, District 77 English teachers had convinced administrators and the local school board to purchase a complete set of textbooks for grades 7 through12. The publishers of the texts had sent representatives to help a group of English teachers. Together they had spent a year reviewing the new instructional model and debating it. Inella Burns, chair of the English Department, was widely respected in the district, and her judgment weighed heavily on the outcome.

The committee decided that although it clarified much of the ambiguity from the traditional model, it was no simpler. Its success depended largely on a staff development program. The administration agreed to pay an instructor to teach the staff the model but not pay teachers for time spent. I wanted the training. I had taught traditional grammar without proper preparation, and I didn't want to repeat that experience.

Hilja Karvonen, a linguist at Mankato State would instruct us. Acting more like a group of Methodists than educators, teachers hosted sessions in their homes and Hilja presented the sessions as we drank coffee and munched on treats. All went smoothly.

Attendance was good, comprehension seemed adequate and by all appearances we were headed toward a successful launch of the new teaching model.

Alas, it was a flop. Students were unable to grasp the concepts. Teacher's found themselves combining traditional and transformational grammar. Within a year the new books had been relegated to the bookrooms.

Although some of the concepts were helpful in explaining grammar, the time and effort spent outweighed any gains. The publishers probably had not used enough students in their research and development—an oversight that happens in all businesses. Constant monitoring of new programs is needed to determine their effect. Also helpful would be testing new textbooks in one classroom for a year before investing in a 7 through 12 purchase.

Professional Conferences

In 1969 I was given the opportunity to attend the National Council of Teachers of English Convention in Atlanta. The first three days I spent with New York University professor Neil Postman who had just written *Teaching as a Subversive Activity* and was considered the most innovative and controversial educational thinker in the country.

He and others who attended his seminar, stretched my mind. Ray Lemley who taught humanities in New Haven, Conn. and Art Daigon, an English professor at the University of Connecticut were among them. They shared ideas for revolutionizing teaching that focused heavily on the impact of media on students. Postman was Orwellian in his belief that media, not reading, would be the driving force in the lives of students. He said, "If teachers do not prepare students to dig truth from the distortions that are presented by the media moguls, our way of life is threatened."

Postman altered my views on the English curriculum. I worried less about the parts of speech and more about interpretative viewing and reading. It seemed apparent that helping students understand the use and impact of media propaganda was vital to preparing students to live successfully.

At the convention I also was able to preview materials and share ideas with dedicated teachers from throughout the nation. I flew home with suitcases filled with instructional materials and sources that could be used to improve my own curriculum.

Mentoring Student Teachers

In 1975, when my principal assigned me to teach three sections of 8th grade anthrohistory, I said, "What's that?"

"You're about to find out, " he answered.

Somehow, when writing the curriculum, the eighth-grade social studies teachers decided to include this funny, little hybrid. It included the study of the evolution of humanity, early man's culture and the progression to his modern day culture. It also seemed to include whatever else the teacher chose to teach.

There were several resource texts but no primary text. Teachers picked and chose what they wanted and taught the students bits and pieces. For many of us it was a frightening course and as with English grammar and gymnastics, I was among the frightened. Once again I found myself only one day ahead of my students. It seemed to be my fate.

This time, though, I had two advantages. There would be no Sue's in any of my classes because none of the students knew anything about early man. Also my good friend, Errol Villa, who taught the subject, was a willing resource. The first year I struggled. The second year I was assigned a student teacher. As always, I protested. "How can I help a student teacher; when I know so little?"

The protest was futile and Jim Cummings, a history major; and an anthropology minor, was to be my mentee. When we met, his enthusiasm to get started was pleasing. He had a soft spoken gentle manner and a wealth of experience. "Roger, I have lots of ideas and some tools to share with the students. I have participated in an archeological dig, I own my own tepee and have lived in it, and I have made primitive tools and used them. Will I be allowed to set up lab experiences where students make and use the tools implemented by early man?"

In no time Jim and I were off to the races. To prepare for the lab we bought obsidian to make arrowheads, found deer antlers to use as shapers, walked through forests seeking properly shaped branches to make atl-atls, found squirrel and rabbit hides to scrape and prepare, and got large cardboard boxes to make into elephants. Next, we got permission to "plant" artifacts in the high jump pit where we planned to conduct an archeological dig.

Under Jim's tutelage I practiced making arrowheads at home. We broke small chunks from the larger piece of obsidian trying to shape it into our final product. While Jim created excellent imitations, mine were crude. I would have been the laughingstock of the tribe.

On a beautiful spring day, Jim set up his teepee on the small; grassy knoll outside Lincoln. A short distance away, our cardboard elephants roamed the plains. Our atlatls, hides, and obsidian were spread around the grass. Jim demonstrated how to break off chunks of obsidian and shape them into arrowheads.

Next he next took the students to the hunting grounds and showed them how to use the atlatl. He placed his spear on the end of the curved branch, holding it there until with a powerful, quick motion, he hurled it at the cardboard elephant penetrating the rear quarter of his prey.

For the next several days we assigned students to different stations. Each hurled the atlatl, made arrowheads, scraped and prepared hides and spent time in the teepee, where Jim explained how Native Americans lived. My ability to teach the anthrohistory course grew immensely.

Sandy Schwartz was another excellent student teacher. Usually I required one week of lesson plans in advance. I reviewed them on Fridays and observed the results in the classroom the following week. Sandy insisted on reviewing the results of the plan at the end of every day and modifying the next day's plan based on those results.

Sandy was a skilled organizer and my mayhem system drove her crazy. She organized and color-coded all of my files of tests, study guides, and compositions. Each task she was assigned was completed with the same intensity that Andy Griffith applied when he was the permanent latrine orderly in the movie, *No Time for Sergeants*.

Flexible–Modular Scheduling

During the late 1960's and early 1970's as teachers struggled to improve student learning, educational theorists, although late to the table, attacked the problem as well. Some consensus developed among them. They theorized that if students had more choice in selecting their daily curriculum, they would perform better. Administrators were to develop a school day with a larger number of periods. This varied from 12 to 19. Each morning students would select which classes they wanted to attend.

These classes would not be lectures or discussions classes but periods when teachers would assist with students projects. New schools built to accommodate this model would have a few large classrooms where presentations, films and guest speakers might present information that was common to all student's educational needs. Most classes would be held in smaller rooms which were designed for more individualized or small group arrangements. Students there would be would be helped by instructors in completing their projects.

Students in English 10 for example, with the guidance of their instructor, could write a paper on humor in Shakespeare's tragedies or a physics student may build a model bridge from toothpicks. If a student chose to spend three 20 minute periods or mods on the bridge project on Monday and none on Tuesday, that was their choice. This way, students would play a much larger role in the design of their own education. Developers of this this model believed that over time the students would become skilled in this process. They would become partners to teachers and all would benefit.

John J. Nelson, the principal at Lincoln, was a true conservative. He hated nothing more than change. While other schools were experimenting with the idea, he ridiculed it. "Students choosing what classes they're going to attend is nonsense," or "don't those damn fools know anything about kids? I think they're afraid of them. They want to let 12-year-olds run the world."

Dr. Glines, the principal at Wilson, the Mankato State laboratory school, decided to go full bore with the model. The local newspaper reported encouraging stories. My friend Warren Mickelson and I visited Hosterman Junior High in Anoka to examine its model and came home underwhelmed. Teachers had no idea which students or how many would be at any of the 19 modules a day. Detention rooms were packed. Students were skipping classes, and chaos reigned. The police were called to break up fights among students roaming around outdoors. Notifying parents where their students were during the day was almost impossible.

Still the media and theorists continued to praise the model. In Mankato the administration and school board moved cautiously. The compromise at Lincoln included the development of an independent study period and shortened class times. Students signed up in the morning where they planned to attend I.S. In theory it made sense.

If they needed more help on their English assignment they might choose their English teacher for independent study. In practice, it didn't work that way. Students quickly determined which teachers gave them the most freedom.

Few students signed up for my independent study because I required them to work on my assignments. My colleague across the hall had students spilling out the doorway because his requirements were less stringent. To attract more students, I developed mini-courses on subjects like "A Cheap and Easy Explanation of Football." I, and many other teachers, had these mini-classes on Fridays and enjoyed large audiences, but they did little to promote scholarship within the curriculum.

Mankato East High School was built during this period. The walls between its classrooms were designed to slide open for large group instruction and slide shut for small groups. The fad faded and the thin, porous walls remain.

Allowing the media and politicians to solve problems in education continues to hinder progress in meeting student's needs. This period of reform was followed by an attempt to force teachers to develop their teaching skills.

Licensure Renewal Units

In 1965 when I accepted a position in the Mankato Public Schools, teachers with no-life certificates were required to earn six college credits every four years in the subject they taught. That was the sum total of the staff development program.

In the early 1970's, the policy was revised. The college credits were increased from 6 to 12 or an alternative plan could be sent to the personnel director's office for approval. Guidelines for the plan included such things as approved educational research, attendance at appropriate workshops or conferences and papers developed from those conferences.

Teachers with life certificates didn't have to meet those requirements. The legislature then enacted a bill ending the issuance of life certificates but I still had one. Just as I had in high school basketball, I sat on the sidelines and watched as teachers wrote alternative in-service plans and were denied approval. This time, though, I was pleased to be sitting out the game.

During the years I was at Lincoln our leaders experimented with reform with varying success.

Staff Development Coordinators

Mankato School District 77 took a giant step forward in its commitment to continuing education for its teachers when it implemented a staff development model that included adding two full-time development coordinators. The model was a partnership between Mankato State University and the district. They shared both the costs and the benefits. At the University the coordinators were responsible for placing and training student teachers. In the school district coordinators were responsible for training the teaching staff best teaching practices.

The old model, which considered six graduate credits adequate, was abandoned. Implementation of instruction in best practices was now monitored by coordinators, which seemed a daunting task for them.

When Ben Buck, the college administrator responsible for supervising this new model, first posted the development coordinator job, I considered applying for it. I had come to know Ben through his wonderful daughter, Beverly, who had been my student. I discussed the job with him, and he was encouraging, even though I didn't meet all the requirements. In the end, I didn't apply, Sheryl's health and my family responsibilities were the main factor in that decision.

Jim Keckeisen and Pat Reichel were selected to fill the positions and both were excellent. I believe their work resulted in improved instruction in the district.

Human Relations Training

In 1975 the Minnesota Department of Education required all teachers without life certificates complete a course in human relations. This was to ensure that teachers were sensitive to special needs students. Multi-culture, gender, and disability issues were covered.

Two major problems developed as these courses were implemented.

First teachers felt insulted by the mandate. They believed it insinuated they were insensitive to these issues. Second, many felt it was heavy handed in its delivery.

At these classes members of these minority communities seemed to place blame for their problems on teachers. Sometimes they were explosive and vitriolic in the presentation of their message.

Summary of Experiences 1965-1977
What I Learned

From 1965 until 1978 my life wasn't typical for a young parent and teacher. Distractions outside the classroom were major. Although my love of teaching was still strong, my life circumstances affected my teaching and stole from the time and effort necessary to strengthen my professional development.

The controversy over the Viet Nam War had a profound impact on the school. John J. Nelson, the Principal, met university students at the front door of the school and told them, "This is a school. I am responsible for the safety of these children while they are here. Leave immediately."

Sheryl and I were barely able to meet our financial responsibilities on my $5,800.00 salary, so Sheryl began working evenings and weekends at Thro Drug, selling cosmetics. When we purchased our home, with the assistance of Sheryl's mother, Sheryl accepted a teaching position eight miles from Mankato in St. Clair. It proved to be a fulfilling experience for her and gave us the necessary income to consider enlarging the family.

The district summer school program also helped our finances. Because of a scheduling conflict between band and history, most high school students studied history in an accelerated six-week, four hour-a-day program. Summer school teachers were compensated with two-thirds of their daily pay. Classes were filled with motivated students whom it was a joy to teach.

The district used an application process to fill the positions and there were more applicants than vacancies. I was fortunate to be offered a position the first year I applied. That didn't sit well with Pat Flynn, the chief negotiator and union representative. He saw me as an English teacher who was reaching too far beyond my area of expertise and told me so. A summer long battle ensued, but I completed my job in spite of it. Eventually Pat and I became friends as we found our social and political views were far more alike than different.

In 1969 I completed my master's degree in English. My thesis was titled *Religion in the Novels of Ole Edvart Rolvaag*. Although, my advisor, Dr. Hjalmer Lokensgaard, was impressed neither with the subject nor the quality of my research, the process was intense, and I was relieved it was finished. My respect for higher scholarship and my paycheck increased as a result.

In 1970 we adopted our son, David, and Sheryl resigned her job to stay home with him and Shelly. We purchased a larger home at 304 Emerson Lane. Sheryl did homebound instruction for the Mankato Schools to supplement our income, and I became a partner with my colleague and friend, Errol Villa, in a real estate investment. With no money down, we bought an old dilapidated duplex at 712 North 5th Street repaired it and rented it out.

The ship of life appeared to be sailing smoothly. Then in 1972 Sheryl was stricken with diabetic-induced kidney failure. Before this her type I, childhood-onset diabetes, had been little more than an inconvenience. Now, for the next three years, we battled the demons of her illness. These included wildly fluctuating blood sugar, overwhelming exhaustion, and frequent emergency hospitalizations. Late night trips to Methodist Hospital in Rochester were frequent. The children grew accustomed to going to bed with Sheryl and I at home and waking up with Grandma Preston.

On April 11, 1975, following a visit with her aunt in Florida, Sheryl died at home from elevated blood sugar levels.

The next year I was granted a sabbatical and enrolled in the graduate counseling program at Mankato State. This gave me time to grow accustomed to being a single parent to Shelly and David, to mourn the loss of Sheryl, to adjust to my new responsibilities and to manage graduate school.

Under the tutelage of my advisor, Dr. Jack Auger, I acquired the counseling skills necessary to assist students struggling with problematic lives, to resolve some of the anxiety and sadness issues that plagued me, and to move forward with my family responsibilities.

The Villas and I also purchased more property that needed refurbishing. Although in retrospect it seems ill advised, the accompanying mental and physical demands kept me occupied. Brooding over the hand I had been dealt, may have been worse.

With the help of Sheryl's mother, my parents and some professional counseling, I was able to keep my head above water during the year after Sheryl's death and I returned to Lincoln in the fall of 1976. I resigned from coaching, but remained a full-time teacher and continued to buy and sell real estate with the Villas.

While I was on sabbatical, the teacher's union had become more militant. Pat Flynn asked teachers to "work to rule." They were to divorce themselves from the school outside contract work hours. That way, school boards across the state were forced to negotiate in good faith.

In the fall of 1976 I realized, that although Sheryl had died, I had not. Forcing myself to try new things, I began to play racquetball at the YMCA, joined a solo parent group, and tried dating. This last was complicated by the fact that since Sheryl's death, my sex drive had disappeared. I never knew whether my date expected a sexual encounter. I knew there wouldn't be one.

Although my depression had lifted, I made an appointment to see a grief counselor. During one visit, he gently laughed as he said to me, "Roger, you're one of those guys who needs to be in love before you have a sexual relationship. Relax, you're going to be all right."

He was right. In March of 1977 I met and fell in love with Beverly Ann and the problem disappeared. During our brief courting period, we spent as much time together as possible. We treasured those moments.

Bev was teaching fifth grade at Hoover Elementary, and I had returned to Lincoln, so both of our lives were filled with responsibilities. In an effort to meet all of them and spend time together each day, we often shared late-evening dinners at Michael's or the Century Club. Keeping all these balls in the air, I was regularly tired during the day. Sometimes my head nodded and I dozed briefly during quiet moments in the classroom. I was convinced the students were unaware of this until the day the caption on my student made current events bulletin board was titled *"Stoufer'Snewz."*

When Bev and I met, we were both planning solo vacations. She was going to Germany, Austria and Switzerland, while I was considering a trip to Kenya. Hers was predicated on her interest in European culture, art, and fashion, while I was curious about the Leakey family's early work on the origin of humanity in the Olduvi Gorge in Kenya. As we talked about our plans, Germany piqued my curiosity, and I chose to travel with Bev. We've been traveling together ever since.

We married August 5th, 1977. It was a joyous day for us, and every day since continues to be. After Sheryl's death I made a vow to God that given a second opportunity to love, I would be a better husband. I promised not to take the simple things in marriage for granted. I have worked at fulfilling that promise.

Marrying Bev returned stability to my life. It was coupled with a newfound enthusiasm for fulfilling all the responsibilities of my job, and an enormous energy. A heightened awareness of the brevity of life made me less risk averse. I found myself willing to explore ventures both inside and outside school that I never would have before.

Bev continued teaching at Hoover Elementary. Our future plans included her resignation so that we could enlarge our family. In the blink of an eye, and with little preparation on my part, my responsibilities changed and grew. The change was precipitated by decreasing enrollment in the district and something I noticed while watching a gathering of Lincoln students outside my room in the late autumn of 1977.

"Holy shit!" I thought. "Those kids are smoking weed within plain sight of me and they don't seem to mind the fact that I see them." I recognized many of them and was aghast at their gall. They were toking up only 15 feet from the school grounds. I knew this required immediate action but I was prepping for classes and the warning bell for the students to be in their classrooms was sounding.

As soon as possible, I followed my typical approach for significant problems and met with Hank Nett, the school counselor. He had the balance and the skill to examine complex problems, break them down and solve them one piece at a time while still keeping the lines of communication open. He would investigate and act appropriately but not until first confirming my suspicions. Hank would find truth. He always did.

Later he and I agreed to use our student networking skills, research the situation, and meet again to determinate the next step. Both of us had developed trust with students who were willing to tell us what happening. We were confident they would tell us all they knew.

The first student I sought out was Mary. After teaching class I asked her to stay. "I thought I saw you hanging around with some kids by that old garage in the alley this morning," I told her.

She haltingly responded, "Not me; I'm not into that stuff."

"What stuff?"

"You know," she said. "Those kids are getting high before school starts. Everybody knows."

When Hank and I met the next day we found that our investigations had resulted in the same conclusions. We needed to inform John J., the principal, and let him work out a plan.

John J. listened carefully as we told him what we had discovered. He concluded by saying, "I'm going to call Herb and Rollie and see if they're experiencing this same crap at Franklin and North Mankato. If our kids are doing drugs before school, I bet theirs are too. It sure as hell caught me off guard. I never expected this would happen in Mankato."

His calls confirmed the problem was epidemic. Principals at the superintendent's monthly meeting voted to develop a district policy including guidelines for administrators to follow during an intervention with students who were using, selling or under the influence of drugs on school grounds.

Superintendent Stark was cautious about policy changes and worried about inaccurate and misleading information becoming public perception. The press always seemed omnipresent when explosive issues like this one surfaced. Fears of the media sometimes curtailed candid discussion of unconventional ideas that may or may not become part of a solution. This meant that the process used to develop the policy would be inclusive, with shared community input and ownership and would follow a very transparent model.

The declining enrollment affected me even more than the drug issue. Enrollment in the elementary schools had been declining for years, and it had finally affected the junior highs. In early May of 1978 John J. came into my room after school. This was unusual, so I knew something was up.

He began, "Don Ruble [the West High School Principal] called me. He has an opening in ninth grade English and he wants you."

"I don't think I want the job," I said. "I'm content here. There's too much politics and squabbling over there. Send Wiltgen. He'd like it there."

"You have no choice," John said. "I don't have enough students enrolled to keep you."

I knew arguing would be futile. I believed he was satisfied with my performance, and was pleased that Ruble had chosen me. I was headed to West High School.

From Lincoln to West

The staff at Lincoln trusted each other, respected each other's skills, and followed orders. They were rarely defiant and didn't venture out of the box much. Classroom culture varied little. Most staff members believed that to be the manner in which schools should operate. If we disagreed with a practice being used, we remained silent.

I was bothered by the use of paddles to discipline students. I first learned of it when Hardean Bonkrude, who taught U.S. history, called me to the door during class. He spoke loudly enough for all the room to hear, "I'd like you to witness as I paddle Joel."

Caught by surprise, I said dumbly, "I'm sorry I don't understand."

He said firmly, "It is the policy in our school that we cannot strike a child in anger. Joel intentionally provoked another student. I am going to paddle him. Another teacher must observe me do this to testify I was not out of control. I want you to witness."

After striking the student twice Bonkrude said, "Thank you, Mr. Stoufer." This was a far cry from the disciplinary procedures used at Stewart.

I didn't like what I had seen. Bonkrude had swung the paddle with such force that when it struck, he nearly lifted the diminutive seventh grade boy from the floor. It seemed brutal and excessive. Eventually, two or three times I did paddle students whose behavior had been extremely inappropriate. I was never comfortable doing it and am not proud to admit having done it.

I was relieved to leave this behind at Lincoln.

Hank Nett

The greatest gift I received from Lincoln Junior High was the mentoring I received from Hank Nett, the counselor. Henry looked like Mark Twain but he could solve mysteries like Sherlock Holmes. He loved the challenge. One day I was leaving school after gymnastics practice. Our 2 year old, was being cared for by a friend, Patty Keitzer, who lived across the street from Lincoln. As I carried Michelle back across Hanover Street someone shouted, "Stoufer sucks."

I drove Shelly home to North Mankato and returned to Lincoln hoping to identity the culprit. Anxious but determined to accomplish my goal, I pounded on the door and rang the doorbell at the same time. It was quieter than a graveyard on a moonless night. "I know you're in there. Stop being cowards," I shouted. There was no response. It was time to go home and plan what to do next.

The next morning I went to Hank's office and told him what had happened. "Let me go to work on this," he said.

During my prep period two hours later he called me back to his office. He had identified the culprits. Two were Lincoln students and the third attended the Catholic school only a few blocks away. We called in the Lincoln kids one at a time and announced their punishment. They would be in after school detention for an hour after school for the next week. I suggested doing nothing about the third kid because I didn't know him.

Hank's response was immediate. "No way! I'll call the nuns and we'll go right over there and visit with him."

Hank was a good Catholic with 11 children of his own. He knew the nuns would cooperate. When we arrived at the school, the principal had the guilty boy in her office. He apologized to me and received the same punishment as the Lincoln boys. The nuns agreed to monitor his detention.

Hank was also skilled at reading between the lines. Once, while meeting with a local lawyer and his wife about their son's lack of academic progress, the teachers and parents began assailing the kid. Hank ended the session quickly and asked me to stay as the others left.

When we were alone he shook his head and said, "Will you take that kid under your wing, Rog? He needs some nurturing."

When I was coaching gymnastics, he sometimes brought a boy to practice and asked, "Can Charlie join gymnastics tonight? I think he has real potential."

Hank never found a great gymnast for our team, but he found those kids some great friends on the team.

Hank's best attribute was the strength of his convictions. When he concluded that one of our female teachers was threatening to the female students she taught, he met with the central administrators and presented the evidence. Then he issued an ultimatum. "Either she goes or I go."

Hank had borrowed my car that day to attend the meeting but rattled by what happened he returned the car to the parking lot but failed to return my keys. Several years after the teacher had been dismissed, he explained why.

I did my best to model what I learned from him but he was always the master.

Errol Villa

Errol was hired to teach social studies at Lincoln in 1969. With our similar backgrounds and interests, we soon forged a strong bond. After summer school we painted houses together and planned for a future partnership investing in rental property. In 1973, when the opportunity to purchase an old duplex with no money down and contract for deed financing became available, we took it.

We bought 20 gallons of incorrectly mixed brown paint at Sears for one dollar a gallon, dumped them all into a 30 gallon garbage can, stirred them together, poured the new color back into the gallon cans, and started beautifying our investment.

The house had been vacant for over a year. Several windows were broken. Used condoms and girls' panties littered the floor of the upstairs bedroom.

Neither of us were glaziers, but we decided to apprentice ourselves to the craft and bought some cheap glass cutters at OK Hardware. The school district was replacing the windows at Lincoln and we received permission to remove the glass from the old windows. Before long we were replacing the glass in the broken windows and enjoying practicing our new skill.

We filled cracks in the old plaster and took advantage of wallpaper sales to cover our hideous craftsmanship. We monkey-matched the paper and admired the almost finished product. Finally, we rented a floor sander from A to Z Rental and removed the layers of old, cracked varnish that covered the floors.

Our first tenant, Bill was a disabled painter who hobbled around on a wooden leg. He loved to tell tall tales, and Errol loved to listen. His favorite tale was usually told after he had drunk a bottle of cheap whiskey mixed with Mountain Dew. "Rotten," [He either never got my name right or he enjoyed calling me his nickname for me] he would say. "I was painting a water tower in Waterloo, Iowa. A gust of wind blew me straight out from the railing. I clung to it till the gale finally tore me loose. I fell over a hundred feet to the ground below. The old gravity force pulled me so powerful that it sucked my left leg into the ground right up to the knee. Some kind folks cut it off right there and saved my life. That's the whole goddamn story, Rotten."

Some days Errol didn't get much done other than talk to Bill. Bill told stories of his investment strategies, his time spent in jail, and his son, Bill Jr., who was serving time in a Federal Penitentiary in Tennessee.

Sheryl and I also socialized with the Villla family. Their children were brilliant and wonderful. Errol loved to sing along at the piano bar at the Century Club or stop for a drink at Michael's and sometimes locked the places up when he left.

Sheryl's illness and death, my new responsibilities and my romance with Bev altered my life style and heightened my awareness of emerging problems in the Stoufer-Villa partnership. I knew my work habits were changing. During our last summer as partners the parting of ways became inevitable. I had become disengaged from the business side of our relationship and sought a simpler life, while he, on the other hand, became more possessive of the business. I arranged a meeting to discuss this with the Villa's, but Errol was not present. His wife, Perci, and I decided it was best to terminate the partnership. Although it went unsaid, I knew it also was the end of this intimate friendship. I felt almost as if a loved one had died. Without Bev, it might have been unendurable.

During the next school year Errol and I shared a student teacher and worked together at Lincoln. To the best of my knowledge, neither the staff nor the students were aware of the situation we had outside school.

John J. Nelson – My Boss

In the spring of 1965 I interviewed for the teaching position at Lincoln with Principal John J. Nelson. After having trouble finding an unlocked door, I was ushered to his office by the custodian, Al Boldt. I introduced myself and waited for a barrage of questions designed to trip me up. It didn't happen. Instead Mr. Nelson began to tell me about the quality staff and curriculum at Lincoln. I nodded and listened for nearly 30 minutes. Occasionally he asked me a question. Finally he informed me, "I will recommend your appointment to Mr. Nigg. He may wish to visit with you before the final approval is given." Superintendent Nigg never arranged an interview. The job was mine, and Mr. Nelson was my new boss.

His priorities were clear at our first staff meeting "Be on time. Don't leave your classroom unattended. Always monitor the halls between classes. Do not bring unimportant issues to the principal's office. Keep your room clean. Be certain the shades are pulled to an even height after school. Don't miss work unless it's critical. Don't leave the building during the school day. Any violation of these rules will result in consequences. Do all of these and teach your classes well and I will be very supportive of you."

That, in a nutshell was John J. Nelson. He was a no frills, get the job done guy.

Memorable Teachers

Dolores Greely

Dolores Greeley [Grizzly] was one of the most creative teachers I ever knew. She could find a solution to almost any problem that interfered with students succeeding in their reading.

Grizzly had a variety of roles at Lincoln, but I worked most closely with her when she was the reading consultant. I was teaching Pygmalion and my students were struggling with the cockney dialect. They had managed to drop the h's but were unable to read the rest. I told Grizzly about it and she said, "Give me your text, and I'll work up a lesson or two that we can team-teach.

The next day, dressed for the role, she stood in front of the class and in perfect cockney dialect introduced herself as Eliza Doolittle.

"Ow the eck r ya?" she said. In minutes she had placed the students in groups, giving them scripts in dialect, and had them reading to each other. She and I moved around the room participating with each group as they practiced.

She spent the next two days in my room teaching the language, history and culture. She held a contest to select the best cockney speaker in each class. She concluded by clarifying the role of language as a major determinant of social and economic positions in society.

Dolores multiple skills and talents and her ability to build trust with us allowed her to teach the teachers too teach.

Eldon Peterson

If the test of time is the gold standard in determining value, Eldon "Pete" Peterson has earned a top ranking in history or at least the history of his students at Lincoln Junior High. Students he taught 30, 40, or even 50 years ago still say, "How is Mr. Peterson? He was the best teacher I ever had."

Frequently they say things such as, "He had high standards and he held me to them. I performed at a level on his fitness test that I didn't think was possible," or "He taught me to be a leader. He made me believe I had the skills and qualities essential for leadership. He deserves a great deal of credit for my success today." And "I always knew Mr. Peterson cared about me. I was poor but he treated me the same as the kids whose families were rich and ran the town."

While coaching football Pete was competitive but he never let winning be more important than participating. Pete made certain everybody on the team played in every game.

Each evening after practice we prepared the next day's lesson plan for practice. Under Pete's leadership all skills were practiced and all players were prepared physically and mentally to play.

John Dorn

John spent only one year teaching at Lincoln and he would be the first to admit it wasn't his best. His second year in the district he was assigned to Mankato East High School. It was there that he fine tuned his performance and moved to first chair in a field of skilled instrumentalists. He managed his classroom in such a manner that the melody and harmony were always present. When dissonance was heard, he calmly rewrote the score to eliminate it.

I met John when he visited my classroom. He was student teaching at Mankato High School and had been sent to observe my junior high classes. The students were writing poetry and he joyously joined them. By the end of that day we were friends.

John was unabashed in his use of trickery to hold students interest. Smoke and mirrors were among the tools he used. He always had a bowl of M&M's on his desk. If a student's response to a particularly difficult question was detailed and they supported their thoughts with documentation of facts and references to solid sources, they were awarded with an M&M.

John served as student activities advisor at East where he chaperoned dances every Friday night throughout the winter months. He also was known for involving staff and students in pep-fests that rocked the building.

When John was elected to the state legislature, he carried the vote in the East boundaries by a sizeable margin. He continued to teach when the legislature was not in session. By doing this the 20 years that he served, he remained grounded and provided true expertise to the legislators, when they were considering legislative proposals related to education.

The same skills that worked for him in the classroom made him a successful legislator.

Memorable Students

Mark Taylor

In the 1950's and 1960's Brett's Department Store was to Mankato what Macys was to New York and Dayton's to Minneapolis. It sold almost everything to everybody. It was the place where shoppers met friends, both by design and by accident. At some point in their life, almost everyone in town had worked there or knew someone who did. Mark Taylor's father owned and operated Bretts.

Being a member of one of the most prestigious families in town might have most kids a bit uppity—not Mark. He was a happy-go-lucky kid who fit everywhere. He understood and practiced inclusiveness long before it became mandated. He was everybody's friend.

When Sheryl's illness became public knowledge, Mark was a leader of the student council at Mankato High School. He, Eric Spore and other council members planned a winter carnival celebration for the students. Unbeknownst to me, they included a fund raiser to financially assist my family with Sheryl's medical expenses.

After the the carnival Mark and Erik arranged to meet us at our house where they presented us a check for over two-hundred dollars. They also brought a loaf of homemade bread. To us, it was the bread of life.

Mark is now a gynecologist at the Mankato Clinic. Much of his extensive community service is performed in our public schools, where among other things he heightens the student's awareness of the dangers of STD's.

When I was elected to the school board I received several congratulatory notes. His still warms me as I read it "I believe, as you taught us in *Animal Farm*, that power corrupts and absolute power corrupts absolutely. I know you will not be corrupted by it. Thanks for your willingness to serve."

Cindy Hakes

Cindy's Hake's family and mine attended Centenary United Methodist Church. Her father, Gordy, was our head basketball coach at Mankato High and her mother, Hazel, was the director of our youth choir at church. They were like a real life Cleaver family from *Leave it to Beaver* fame. Cindy had a beautiful; soprano voice and sang solos both in the church and school choirs. She performed in plays and shared her joy of life with audiences throughout Mankato.

When I taught *Animal Farm* to ninth graders, I required a related project to earn an A on the unit. The final choice on the list was "Design a project of your own that meets my approval." Cindy and her friends did just that. They wrote and performed a skit in which they played different animals from the novel and sang the animal anthem *Beasts of England* that had been written by the pigs. They sang it in their best animal voices. The pigs oinked and the shep bahed.

They proudly kept me apprised of their progress almost daily. Finally, on the day before the performance, Cindy asked, "Mr. Stoufer, May we please perform our skit on the stage on the auditorium?"

I was hesitant but agreed to see what I could do.

Taking this as a yes Cindy asked next. "May we practice in the auditorium tonight after school?"

I agreed, with the caveat that rehearsal had to end at 4:30 because I had to pick up my daughter, Shelly. Cindy was satisfied.

We met after school on the auditorium stage. The girls put on their animal costumes and Cindy directed the play. It was a hoot. When the animals sang, *Beasts of England*, I burst into laughter.

As with all artists, the creative juices kept flowing throughout the rehearsal. At 4:20, when I was ready to leave, the performers were only halfway through their rehearsal. Once again Cindy made a request. "I know you need to leave, but can't we stay and practice?"

She assured me they would clean up, turn off the lights and cause no trouble." At first I said, "NO" but then relented. What could go wrong? I thought.

The next morning when I entered the building, I was overwhelmed by the strong odor of burned wood. I followed it to the auditorium where I saw that the oak flood lights had been badly burned. Oh my God! What happened?

I turned to leave and met Cindy. She was in tears. "Mr. Stoufer, I'm so sorry. We decided to use the footlights. We lifted them open and had a hard time finding the switch to turn them on. We closed them when we left. I thought we'd shut them off." She paused weepimg. "What do we do now?"

I said, "Cindy, It's my fault, I didn't do my job. I'm not to leave students unsupervised. I'll report what happened to Mr. Nelson."

"I'll go with you if you want."

"No, it'll be better if I'm alone."

The odor was too strong for the performance that day but the cast received a standing ovation for it in my classroom.

Every year when Cindy returns to Mankato with her family for the holidays, I have enjoyed reminiscing and laughing with her about this incident. She has been involved in Christian missionary work all of her adult life. The lights still get a little brighter whenever she enters a room.

Roberta

Success is sometimes difficult to measure. I first met Roberta September 11, 1974, when I was coaching eighth-grade football at Lincoln. The practice field was three blocks away at West High School. The players suited up at Lincoln and walked. My mentor and fellow coach, Eldon Pederson, usually drove us to and from practice in his 1951 Chevrolet. If there was an injury we would need the car. I always left my black 1969 VW fastback in the parking lot at Lincoln.

One day, as Pete and I returned to the parking lot he exclaimed, "Doggone it Coach, all the tires on your car are flat."

"Damn," I muttered. "It's my wife's birthday and we have dinner plans in an hour."

I called Sheryl to tell her I would be late and quickly showered. Pete took me to a service station where I borrowed an air tank to fill my tires. The problem was resolved in an hour and although our dinner was a bit later than planned, we celebrated Sheryl's birthday.

The next morning when I arrived at school, I was on a mission. I was determined to figure out who let the air out of my tires. I told John J. our principal, and his first question was, "Did you have any confrontations with students yesterday?"

"No, my classes this year are great," I said. "I can't think of anyone who has a motive."

John thought for a moment, "Let me do a little research."

Later, during my prep hour, he called me and said, "Roger, I've got the culprit here in my office. Do you want me to send her to your room or do you want to visit with her in my office?"

"Her?" I thought.

"I'll do better than that," he said. "I'll bring her down to make sure she doesn't take off."

I couldn't believe my eyes. She was about four feet eight and her red hair was unwashed with rooster tails spiking randomly. Despite the eighty degree temperature, she wore a plaid flannel shirt and dirty blue jeans. Before John could speak, she smiled, a bit like Gilly on Saturday Night Live, and said, "Sorry."

I was speechless, the planned lecture vanished. "I don't even know you," I blurted out, "Why did you let the air out of my tires? Who are you?"

She looked down and whispered, "I'm Roberta."

Berta lived only a block from Lincoln. Although she attended the school, she was in none of my classes. Her act of mischief was random, and I happened to be the victim. She was one of Errol's students next door.

Errol and I had bought some fixer-upper houses near Lincoln only two blocks from Berta's home. We planned to rehab them the following summer. That is when Berta became almost a daily part of my life.

Her parents were divorced, and she lived with her mother, who had few rules for her and, in a word, was quite eccentric. Berta, like Topsy, "just growed up." Nobody really raised her. She was a wild, untamed creature unhindered by the rules of life that would normally apply to a thirteen-year-old girl. Even so, Berta, to the best of my knowledge, didn't drink, smoke, or spend time with boys.

In April of 1975 I was widowed. With all that was happening probably the last thing I needed in my life was a responsibility like Berta. But that summer she proclaimed squatter's rights on the home on Lewis Street that Errol and I were preparing for sale. She was usually there when we arrived in the morning and stayed until we left in the evening. As we painted and hung wallpaper, she cleaned up behind us. We never officially hired her, but we regularly fed her and paid her. And like a stray kitten, she stayed near us.

She helped us load lumber at the lumberyard, ate hamburgers with us at Hardees and came along when we brought windows to the OK Hardware store to be repaired. Often we encouraged her to hang around with people her own age but she would have none of it. Her loyalty was deep and lasting. Two years later, she was actually watching when I gave Bev her engagement ring.

Bev first met Berta at a duplex I was painting near Lincoln. When Bev pulled up in her car, Berta, wanting to impress her, popped and held a wheelie on her bicycle, down the center of Pleasant, a busy one-way street. As she rode, cars were backed up behind her. I watched in horror as she pulled too hard on the handlebars and fell flat on her back, her head slamming against the asphalt. Cars drove around her as Bev rushed over. I made a halfhearted effort to direct traffic and prevent a larger tragedy. As Bev bent over her, Berta pulled her long red hair over her eyes to hide the tears.

She was back at work the next day. She helped me assemble some scaffolding I needed to paint the 24-feet-high high peak of the house. I laid planks across the top layer of scaffolding to serve as a floor while I painted and then left for the day.

The next morning when I arrived I checked the scaffolding's strength by shaking it a little at the bottom. Berta shouted down from the top; "Knock it off." She had spent the evening sleeping there under the stars.

It was then that Bev decided Berta needed to be domesticated. School was about to open, and Bev wanted Berta dressed like the other girls. She took her to Brett's Department store and bought her blue jeans and a burgundy velour sweater to wear on the first day of school. We never knew whether she chose her faded jeans and plaid flannel shirt or the clothes Bev bought her.

As Berta grew up, our role in her life changed. We moved to the lake making it more difficult for her to drop in. Unexpectedly though, she would reappear in our lives. She married and when her first baby boy was born, she brought her new treasure to our home to share him with us.

About five years ago Berta stopped at our business in Vernon Center. The little baby was now in junior high and had been suspended from riding on the school bus. She sought my advice on how to reverse the decision. When I told her that was unlikely, she accepted it and we moved on to other topics.

She looked at me and said, "Do you and Bev ever smoke pot?"

I laughed loudly and said, "Berta, I can hardly drink a whole beer. Bev and I have never smoked pot and we're too old to start."

Her eyes moved to the floor as they had the first time I met her and she said, "You guys should really try it. Sex is so much better after you smoke a joint." She hadn't changed.

Peter Crosby

Once, when I was explaining the importance of selecting meaningful verbs to strengthen a sentence, there came a knock at my classroom door. Interrupting class was frowned on at Lincoln, so concerned, I quickly moved to answer it.

The interruption proved brief and after a minute I returned to the lesson. Before I could say a word, my students broke into laughter. I glanced at the zipper on my slacks. It was closed, so again I returned to the lesson only to hear more laughter. This time one of the students pointed to a cold air return behind me. When I turned I saw a pair of feet hanging down. Laughing, I said, "Whoever's hiding in there, come on out."

Peter Crosby, the youngest son of the Episcopalian priest slid down. His face was dusty but he smiled as he apologized. "I'm sorry Mr. Stoufer. I intended to return to my seat before you came back. I just crawled up the opening to see what was at the top."

The class was very quiet as they awaited my response, but Peter's charm disarmed me. That seemed to happen a lot with Peter.

Christie Sherwood

I regularly encouraged students to think creatively in their projects so that they could better absorb the lesson and apply its meaning to their lives. When the class was reading *The Chosen,* one student brought his father to share his experiences as a prisoner of war in Germany during World War II. Another student created a collage of pictures of Jewish prisoners held in concentration camps while a third created a crossword using Yiddish slang words.

In ninth grade poetry, Christie Sherwood, asked if she could perform an interpretive dance to explain *The Fiddler of Dooney* by William Butler Yeats while her friend, Pamela Anderson, read the poem. The reading was perfectly matched with Christie's dance. Afterward Christie explained how the dance reflected the poem's meaning. The class was deeply impressed.

Every year for the next three years, until she graduated from West, Christie called to arrange a time to perform her dance for all my English classes. She relished the opportunity to share her love of dance.

The Fiddler of Dooney
When I play on my fiddle in Dooney,
Folk dance like a wave of the sea;

Overhead Era

My cousin is priest in Kilvarnet
My brother in Mocharabuiee.

I passed my brother and cousin;
They read in their books of prayer;
I read in my book of songs
I bought at the Sligo fair.

When we come to the end of time
To Peter sitting in state
He will smile on three old spirits,
But call me first through the gate.

For the good are always the merry...

A Tale of a Teacher

VHS VIDEO TAPE ERA

West High School, Mankato, MN 1977-1991

Go West Young Man, Go West

This place is what I'd dreamed about;
It's fast paced, and lively too.
My assignments are so varied though,
it's somewhat like a zoo.

After twelve years behind a desk at Lincoln, my work life had grown comfortable. Interactions with staff and administration were predictable. Any bumps that arose were avoidable or manageable. The routine wasn't exciting but it was secure. For me Lincoln was a comfortable, old passenger train and West was a fighter plane.

West's enrollment numbered about 900 and its staff 100. Occasionally one or two staff members would leave and one or two would replace them. Everyone—staff and students—seemed more assertive at West. In the lounge, ideas bounced off the walls smacked

159

like tennis balls driven randomly from one racket to another. Teachers at Lincoln played cribbage, read the paper and snacked; West was a beehive of football pools, Asimov quizzes, and pranks.

Salary negotiations always heated the atmosphere some at Lincoln, but West became a tropical rainforest. The year the school board insisted on implementing a discipline policy for teachers, things reached a boiling point at West. Even though salaries, the calendar, benefits and all other contractual considerations had already been agreed on, a settlement had been delayed. Although the discipline clause seemed unnecessary and unappealing to me, I found it less objectionable than many of my colleagues. When it was finally accepted, it divided the staff. Those who had opposed it, refused to let it go.

If the discipline clause split the building, the smoking ban tore it apart. In 1980 Roger Hansen, a science teacher, made a motion at the opening-day workshop to ban smoking in the lounge. Roger had quit smoking during the summer and wanted to avoid it. That motion lit a fuse.

Marty Wiltgen took the floor and asked angrily, "Who the hell do you think you are? If you don't like the smoke in the lounge don't come into it."

"The smoke from the cigarettes drifts into the halls and stinks up the entire area. Students hold their nose as they walk by."

After twenty minutes, Principal John Barnett called for the vote. By a razor-thin margin the motion carried, but the controversy had just begun.

The smokers claimed squatter's-rights in a first floor room. Teachers who used the space as their office were evicted. That space proving too confining, the smokers moved to an empty storage room in the bowels of the annex. They painted it blue, filled it with shabby furniture and ash trays, and settled in.

The Westies also took pride in bedeviling their principal. Pranks like sodding his office floor, replacing his desk chair with a toilet stool and advertising a sale on Christmas trees using his telephone number were common and celebrated in the lounge.

Student activities were available for nearly every interest. Sports, music, drama, debate, science, mechanics, conservation, leadership, government and language were a part of school life. Teachers and students alike were required to make all the programs successful. The best was always homecoming. The coronation, the parade, and the 50th class reunion were all regal. Administrators and teachers performed admirably.

But at the end of each school day my first year at West, I was confused and bored. I taught five sections of English 9 that year. The 10th or 11th time I was asked, "What do you mean when you say a verb sets the time of the action in the sentence?" I found it difficult to remain engaged. I needed more variety and a more challenging schedule. Thankfully, I was newly married. My mind was preoccupied with what I would do after school, helping the classes to pass more quickly.

So it was heartening when assistant principal, Marion Powers called that summer and told me I would now be teaching two sections of

American literature and three sections of English 9. Although I craved variety, my second year at West provided more of it than I expected.

The American literature classes were a perfect fit for my skills. U.S. history was the core of my history major. Finally, I was teaching the classes I had trained for. Anthrohistory and gymnastics, I thought, were part of my past, not my future.

Then, John Barnett informed me that he had dropped two sections of English 9 from my schedule and added two sections of modern media. I had not taken a single course in media. I replied, "The only thing I know about media is what I see on the ten o'clock news."

"That places you ahead of the rest of the English department." he retorted.

When I examined my class roster for modern media in the fall, there were 31students in each section, none of them "the cream of the crop."

Fortunately, my friend Pat Ryan had taught the course, and he shared his expertise and materials with me. He had seen the roster and brought assistant principal, Tom Brekke to visit the class. They both smiled and later said to me, "You got them all."

But, to my surprise, I grew fond of the class. We studied newspapers, television and film. We scripted, storyboarded, and shot short films. Students became adept at creating special effects. They learned that a film was created by splicing 3 to 7 second shots together and that when editing they could use a dummy shot to replace their friend, when their friend was thrown over the edge of a ramp.

Wednesdays were newspaper day. Student assigned selections were required to write explanations for questions raised by the articles. They sat in a circle and challenged each other's written opinions. They were given credit both for sticking to their opinion and for changing their minds, when it was warranted.

Although teaching modern media had already upended my routine, I discovered I was in far more upheaval when John Barnett asked me to be the drug czar at West.

Substance Abuse Program

Illegal drugs were being sold and used at West by a small number of students. In 1980 John Barnett was serving as an interim for principal, Don Ruble who was on sabbatical completing his doctorate. In September, Barnett arranged a meeting with me. He nearly knocked my socks off when he said, "Several students who have completed drug and alcohol treatment programs have asked my permission to hold support group meetings. I believe you completed the counseling program at Mankato State while on sabbatical. John Nelson tells me you helped develop guidelines and a program to assist students with these issues at Lincoln. Are you willing to serve as an advisor to this student group at West?"

"I need time to think about that."

"If you decide to do this I'll free you from supervision duty as compensation for your time and skills. Does that make it more tempting?"

"I'm interested, but I'll need to discuss it with Beverly."

"We are also forming a committee to develop a district policy on student use of mood altering substances. I would like you to serve on that committee."

That caught my attention. I had served on various English department committees but this was a district policy committee, "I would be glad to do that," I told him.

When the committee was formed, it had twenty members. 10 were school district employees and 10 were community members who had a professional interest and some level expertise on the subject. The community members included social workers, doctors, lawyers, members of Alcoholics Anonymous, the chiefs of the Mankato and North Mankato police department and the head of corrections from both counties.

At our first meeting, Barnett nominated me to chair the committee. The other nominee was Del Johnson, a Blue Earth County chemical dependency counselor. We were both disappointed when I was chosen to lead the committee. I knew it would be time consuming and difficult.

After the meeting Barnett renegotiated his offer to me on the student advisory position. He had played his cards well by flattering me with the nomination. He also added a new caveat. Don Rachut, a counselor at West, would help in getting things started.

Our responsibilities were never clarified. Barnett suggested Rachut and I attend a three day workshop in Owatonna, where we would be trained and examine some models of programs we might use for our group.

Don and I bonded during those three days. We broke bread with former addicts who had undergone treatment six or seven times. We discovered what we were in for. Don also made it clear that he served strictly in an advisory capacity. With the limited time and resources dedicated to its development, the program would be built slowly and likely with some casualties. During the single class period that had been assigned to me for implementing and planning, I was unable to give it the time it demanded.

Barnett suggested I meet weekly with a group of students who had returned from treatment. They included primarily young girls who wanted to develop an AA program at West. Only recovering addicts could attend the meetings and students who had completed the AA steps would sponsor those who had not. I was deemed a clerk and denied attendance at the meetings.

I understood the reasoning, but my contract required me to be present with students under my supervision. Cindy Hakes and her wonderful friends at Lincoln; had taught me what might happen when even the most trustworthy students were left unsupervised. I didn't want to be responsible for the possible consequences.

Don and John Barnett offered me the same assistance Tunee had when I told him there were no literature books in Stewart. "Good luck! You'll figure it out."

I was on a steep learning curve. Much of my time was spent researching successful programs in the state, planning and arranging training sessions for the committee, intervening with students in crisis, doing dependency assessments, meeting with parents, taking students to AA meetings or arranging for Del Johnson, Blue Earth County chemical dependency counselor, to provide interventions. The one-hour-a-day release proved vastly inadequate for the job. Peter was always being robbed to pay Paul.

When it became clear that the district needed to hire a full-time chemical dependency counselor, Dr. Jack Sjostrom, the district's curriculum director met with me to register his objections. He said, "Schools are for education. We cannot do all things for all students."

In the fall of 1980 after one year of meetings, the committee voted to recommend to the school board that the district write a job description for a district chemical dependency counselor and find a candidate for that position. At the board meeting where committee member; Rhoda Olson and I presented the committees plan, Sjostrom spoke against the recommendation and the board unanimously voted it down. The following week I met with John Barnett, resigned as advisor to the AA group and asked to be placed back on the supervision list. He agreed and didn't resist.

The student AA group was dismantled, and Blue Earth County provided Del Johnson as the district assessment analyst. He referred students to AA groups outside the school. Although my professional role was over, I continued to help a small number of students. Del and I developed a solid; professional relationship. Over time all the students were transitioned to Del, and I phased out of the program.

In 1984 the school district signed a contract with Addictions

Recovery Technology (ART), a private substance abuse treatment program. It established budgets and service times for all secondary schools and allowed principals to request emergency services when necessary.

Nineteen years later in 2003, while I served on the school board, a community group tried to establish a Sober School. It was designed to educate students returning from treatment in an environment that reinforced and promoted sobriety. They were to help each other and use other community resources, including Blue Earth County and Nicollet County Human Services, corrections, law enforcement, and private resources like ART. The school board decided to manage the program, but to include all available partners in the community with relevant expertise in its program. The funds for a major portion of this program were contributed privately.

The model that resulted resembled the one that the 1980 policy committee desired. Just as the short-beaked finches that Darwin studied on the Galapagos were replaced by longer-beaked finches who could reach the food supply buried deeper in the bark of the tree, the substance abuse program in the school district needed time to evolve into a district-owned program that was better suited to provide rehabilitation for students.

It takes time for ideas to develop into action. The district's model for helping students with addiction required twenty years to reach its present stage and if funding remains available, it will likely continue to improve. It was necessary for community leaders to recognize the complex and insidious nature of addiction. Also, the AA community needed to study what model might best work in the schools before they shared in funding. The community agencies that were in the business of promoting healthy youth needed to figure out how to work together and education was needed for public attitudes about addiction to change.

I had ended my brief involvement with the program at West feeling both frustrated and sad, because I believed I had failed. Over the years as I reviewed my role in it, I realized that I had been given a difficult assignment without the support necessary to succeed. John Barnett, Don Rachut and I had all sought to help the students, but we weren't Messiahs. But if I thought my role in trying to help at-risk students was over, I was wrong.

After that disappointment, the classroom became the focal point of my work life. I found time to participate in more student activities at West High School. Sports, music, drama, debate, Youth in Government and a wide variety of other activities were available to all who had a vested interest in West.

Shelly's Reality Break

Just when it seemed the sharp curves in the road were smoothing out another unexpected hairpin curve appeared in our family life. Michelle, our 14 year old daughter, experienced a major grand mal seizure.

We were in our living room talking with my old collegue Val Whipple when Shelly's friend, Rene Baker, who was normally unflappable, came racing up the stairs of our split-level home. "Shelly fell out of the chair when we were watching television and she's unconscious!" she screamed. "She needs help!"

Bev, Whip and I flew down stairs, where we found Shelly convulsing on the floor. I had seen students have grand mal seizures but never one this violent. Her head was slamming against the carpet and her face was turning black. I knelt beside her, put my hand under her neck and tried to slip my billfold between her tightly clenched teeth. I wasn't certain this was the right thing to do. It was purely an act of desperation.

After what seemed like an eternity the seizure slowly abated and Shelly's eyes opened. She appeared dazed and confused. We moved her to the nearby sofa, let her rest and then took her to the emergency room. After a brief examination, she was admitted. It was the first step in what was to become Shelly's lifelong disability.

The second step came a few months later when she experienced a psychotic break. She was only 15 years old when the voices started tormenting her. They were mean and threatening. In an effort to subdue them, she would shout or whisper softly to them. She seemed incapable of separating them from reality. Hospitalizations at Saint Joseph's Hospital in Mankato and Methodist Hospital in Rochester followed.

Although I continued to teach it was not the primary force driving my life. Bev and I devoted much of our energy to researching the options that were available to parents of schizophrenic adolescents. We reviewed what forms of treatment were most likely to be successful. We met with doctors and reviewed their advice. We made lists and notes to establish priorities. Once we agreed on a plan, we were given new information and were forced to revisit it.

At one point a Dr. questioned me hinting that I may have sexually abused Shelly. I felt deeply threatened by this terrible accusation.

Eventually, the Dr. told me that a nurse in the psychiatric unit had expressed this concern because some other patients with Shelly's symptoms had been victims of incest. As we reviewed the circumstances of Shelly's life, he became convinced the charges lacked validity.

This falsity was almost more than I could bear. Beverly's steadfast love and support sustained me during those dark days.

Shelly was also confused about her relationship with Bev. She was angry that Sheryl had died, and in spite of Bev's constant demonstrations of love to her, she resented Bev.

With the guidance of our local Mankato physician, we found a therapist who focused on teaching us how to manage the destructive effects of the voices that that haunted Shelly. Using those tools we acquired from him, to help her, Shelly learned to sort out reality from the false messages given to her by the voices. Our lives became more bearable and Bev and I were able to move ahead in our family, work, and community life.

We also proceeded with our plans to adopt a Korean child, and Bev accepted a part-time teaching position in the district.

ESL Students

In October 1981 while I was enjoying a cup of coffee in the school cafeteria at school, Bob Nelson, the district elementary director, sat down next to me and, "I have a perfect part-time job for Bev. We are required to provide English language instruction for non-English-speaking students. More Southeast Asian students are moving into Mankato, and we need to add a part-time teacher of English as a second language. I think Bev would be perfect for this. Why don't you ask her to give me a call?"

Bev and I had decided to sacrifice the financial benefits of her teaching for the benefits David and Shelly would obtain from having her in their lives full time. However, this part-time job might appeal to her. I knew she had the strength, conviction, warmth and skills to be successful and wondered what she would say.

I wasn't surprised when she told me that despite several valid concerns, she had decided to accept the position. She was worried about both the time she might lose with David and Shelly and her lack of training for the job. Her training was in teaching native English speakers to learn reading, math and science. She had to undergo 30 hours of minimal training to prepare for the new job.

Bev was hired for three elementary schools; Jefferson, Washington and Franklin. She quickly recognized the importance of developing a trusting relationship with the families of her students. She visited them in their homes, gained insight into family cultures, enjoyed breaking bread with them, and developed a respect for the efforts being made by the families to succeed in their new country.

She also learned that the families didn't arrive in America without emotional baggage. Terry and her two sisters attended Jefferson. Her father brought two wives to the United States. He convinced immigration officials that one of them was his sister. Her mother was the older wife. Her father went back and forth between his two wives. This family had multiple issues because of this.

At Washington were Goi Nho's twin six year old boys. Our church, Centenary United Methodist, had sponsored their family. They had escaped VietNam after the war with other refugees in a small fishing boat and had been rescued on the sea. Goi had left his wife and three daughters behind because he feared they would be sexually abused during the escape ordeal.

Bev visited our pastor at Centenary to apprise him of the situation with Goi and his family and he referred her to the refugee committee at our church. The district superintendent's wife, Ann Dundas, was on the committee and she was already helping another Vietnamese refugee, Ahn Ngyhen. The associate pastor's wife, Jewel Shannon, was also on the committee. After some research, the committee decided to help bring the rest of Goi's family to Mankato. They sought his guidance on how to proceed.

Bringing the rest of Goi's family to the United States required an intermediary with political connections and money. Bev led the charge to make that happen. The experience gave her insight into the problems faced by new immigrant families that helped in her teaching.

As more immigrants arrived from a variety of countries including

Viet Nam, Cambodia, Thailand, Romania, Sudan, Somalia, and Eritrea, the state Department of Education provided more specific guidelines and established certification requirements for those who wanted to become or remain ESL teachers. Bev spent several summers fulfilling the rigorous demands of the requirements, earning a 3.9 GPA at Hamline.

Her job responsibilities were soon woven into the fabric of our lives and had a profound impact on how I taught all of my students. Bev's teaching extended far beyond the classroom. Often when children arrived they had no place to live, had not received the required inoculations, and lacked clothing and school supplies. When families faced these circumstances, Bev's first call was nearly always to our friend and life insurance agent, Carl Schoenstedt. Carl always knew who to call to locate the assistance we required.

Once, after we had located an apartment for a new family, they needed furnishings. Carl sent us to a friend who was a VietNam vet and owned and operated a mobile home park off highway 22 south of Mankato. When we called, the owner said, "Bring a pickup and a trailer and I'll give them their furniture. We owe them a lot."

Upon our arrival he led us to a mobile home that was filled with new furnishings. "These are all items that the purchasers of new homes replaced. There are beds, mattresses, box springs, tables and chairs, sofas, and almost everything else. Take anything that will help them.

Through Carl, we met countless people like him—people who were anxious to help welcome the immigrant families to their new world.

Bev also involved our entire family in helping with the annual Christmas party and other events like it for her students. David, Chad and I provided transportation to and from the parties. We helped with the games, handed out gifts, served food, and followed orders on other assignments as she kept the 27 students from 15 cultures busy and entertained them with dice games, story reading, bingo, and other activities. On those days Bev turned our home into a cosmopolitan castle. Children from all over the world celebrated living together in a new country that offered them opportunities to maximize their talents.

The gifts Bev received from parents of students included egg rolls, breads, and desserts. We acquired new tastes, and although we retained our desire for lefse and lutefisk, Bev learned to make the new delicacies which we had learned to appreciate. These new foods became regular fare on the Stoufer menu.

The impact of the increased diversity brought by the immigrant families Bev taught was felt in the community as well as in our home. The Mankato that I had reached maturity in during the 1960's was predominantly Caucasian, Catholic and Lutheran, Republican and roast beef American. Suddenly, there were Southeast Asians selling egg rolls from street stands outside their homes, ethnic restaurants were cropping up, multi-colored clothes were common on the streets, and the term "immigrant population" no longer referred to our grandparents and great grandparents. Naturally there were problems that came with our new residents.

As curriculum, staffing, and materials evolved to meet the needs of the new population; teachers, administrators, and researchers also continued to seek better learning tools for all students. Ray Schwinegar, the new superintendent, was convinced that teachers needed more training if they were to succeed with the wide range of students in their classrooms. Many teachers believed he was more interested in building his resume than he was in students' achievements. Regardless, to accomplish his goal, he tasked the entire teaching staff with becoming disciples of educational theorist, Madelaine Hunter.

The Madelaine Hunter Lesson Plan Method

Ray was a devotee to the Hunter "lesson plan" formula for teaching and spent much time and money preparing the entire staff to follow her model. Gifted, special education, elementary, secondary, or ESL, it made no difference. Hunter believed all students learned in the same rhythm. Whatever the subject, the lesson plan fit.

The process was simple. Each lesson began with review. If irony was being taught the lesson opened with a discussion of an already-studied story containing irony.

Next was the anticipatory set. Teachers aroused the student's curiosity with stimulating questions about irony. They might relate a personal experience with a twist in it, share newspaper stories containing irony, or have students talk about ironies in their own lives.

A brief explanation of the lesson's objective followed. The objective might be to demonstrate their understanding of irony by writing a paragraph containing irony. It could be either fact or fiction.

Step four was the instruction. Teachers might lead students through a part of their assignment, with them assisting in its development. They might draft an account of a person who never traveled because he was saving for a trip to his homeland. Finally, after saving all his life, completing all the travel arrangements and purchasing a new wardrobe he is ready to depart. Then a friend arrives at his home to take him to the airport and finds that he has died. The homeland was not where he expected it to be.

Step five was to verify. Students and teachers together determined whether this story met all the criteria that had been established by their definition of irony.

Step six was guided practice. The teacher helped students through the first efforts to write the story.

Finally, students made final corrections to their completed paragraph.

Ray was sold on Hunter and force-fed us training in her method. Much of the staff followed reluctantly. Staff development coordinators Jim Keckeisen and Pat Reichel were given the responsibility of the training. Teachers were given release time and met in groups. The meetings were held at Franklin school in a crowded, stuffy room that was not air conditioned and where the temperature hovered near 90 degrees. There they practiced the method. Jim and Pat were well prepared and did a good job but the teachers believed they were already achieving Hunter's results and were openly resentful of the conditions and the training.

Counselor JoAnne Ballou sat by me at the training and wrote notes and whispered to me throughout the presentation. Her notes which said things like; "This stuff is drier than a popcorn fart," reflected a widespread opinion of the Hunter method.

When Ray abruptly left the district, the Hunter era in Mankato school ended. Most rank-and-file teachers probably incorporated some of Hunter's methods into their daily planning but none would ever admit to it. The few remaining teachers who endured the small, overheated classroom where we were trained are likely still telling each other, "It was a bunch of crap," even though they may not completely believe it.

Site Based Management

In 1990 Paul Beilfuss was our superintendent. He came from a different school of thought than Ray. He believed that if each site practiced self-governance, ideas for a better learning environment would be generated from all members of that school "family."

During his first year he formed a group to develop a self-governance plan. At the first meeting Paul announced he didn't like the word "committee" and said, "Let's name this group something other than a committee." After an hour of discussion on the topic Paul said, "Let's call this group a banana. I like bananas and I don't like committees. "Anybody here who doesn't like bananas"?

In spite of the fact that the banana met in evening sessions, just as was the case with the transformational grammar study, teachers received no compensation. Kennedy Elementary, the meeting site for the rest of the year, hosted the overtime session. Teachers sat at tables in the lunchroom as they outlined the guidelines the district would follow in the site-based decision making process. Thirty of the districts finest teachers spent a full year peeling the banana. They decided that while individual buildings could make plans for using their staff development money, none of them could be implemented without the approval of a central committee.

Once again the naysayers hooted .This time they may have been wrong. Beilfuss is long gone but staff development committees continue to meet and make plans designed to improve the instruction in their buildings. Their plans are reviewed, approved, and revised or denied based on whether or they are deemed worthy. Measurable performance criteria are required, and results are examined at the end of each year. The state has established many mandates but the site-based training was important to Mankato's success in using staff development funds.

Other efforts at staff development followed as new superintendents tried to build their resumes.

Improved Instruction Using Outcome Based Education

Of all the staff development efforts made during my 40 years in education, I believe outcome based education had the most potential to improve student comprehension in all disciplines. It required students to develop a measurable understanding of a discipline's core requirements.

If ninth-graders were expected to learn the eight parts of speech they didn't move on from that unit of study until they could do it. Students who hadn't learned it used different materials, which were drawn from different methods of comprehension, and started over again. The process repeated itself until every student had achieved success. Soon, of course, teachers who had 30 students in their classroom were teaching to 15 or 20 different groups. Each one at a different place in the curriculum. Managing the paper work, the record keeping and the monitoring was an enormous task but the results were measurable and it clarified to students what they must achieve to be successful in each class. OBE places the responsibility for learning on the students and requires them to succeed.

Outcome Based Education was not a district wide program. Assistant Principal, Tom Brekke and a small group of West teachers, including Sue Briney–in special education, Jim Hanneman–in algebra, Diane Olson–in algebra, Jane Schostag–in English, Jack Bengtson– in business education and myself among others gave it a whirl. Sue Briney led the charge. She solicited the funding for training and materials from private sources in the community.

Teacher Developed Staff Instruction

Sandy Kerkhoff

In 1990 Sandy Kerkhoff, a talented and industrious special education teacher at West, proposed and developed an innovative model for special education students. Its goal was to integrate regular and special education classes by integrating twenty per cent of a regular classroom with special education students. These classes were to be team-taught by the regular and special education teachers, with the latter providing added assistance to their students. Preparation periods for the teachers were matched to provide the planning time needed to address the complexities. Students in the classrooms would be unaware of the program.

Cooperative learning groups were implemented to integrate students. These groups were tightly structured. They required full participation; no interrupting, addressing each other by name, chairs arranged in perfect circles, and mutual respect. After students mastered these skills and developed trust they used them in group problem solving on a lesson. The lesson might be a composition that focused on using effective verbs. Students wrote a short paragraph, read it to the group and explained their choice of verbs. The group listened and suggested other possibilities that might have been more effective.

Sandy and I teamed on this model for two years. We did not develop a system to provide empirical evidence of its success but both of us believed both student learning and social skills improved.

Cooperative Mentoring

Jean Jirak/Jane Schostag

Jean Jirak and Jane Schostag, both excellent English teachers, led an effort to develop a mentoring partnership model. They encouraged senior staff members to partner up and advise each other on teaching and management strategies. They knew each teacher had a unique set of strengths and they believed that by sharing these in a non-threatening, non-judgmental manner staff members could broaden their skills and students would benefit. Under their model, partners observed each other and shared teaching strategies. Most English teachers participated, and the unexpected result was increased bonding.

Jean later became a mentor teacher for the district, and Jane was appointed by central administration to lead the district developing the state-mandated graduation rule.

Inclusiveness Plan

In 1991 the State of Minnesota Department of Education required that all schools develop a plan that demonstrated that sincere efforts were being made to provide equal opportunities for all ethnic groups, female students, and the disabled. The schools had to ensure that every group of students felt welcome.

Schools had to provide annual proof of progress in meeting these state-established goals. Every part of the school day from the morning bus ride to school to the basketball game that evening would be involved. Bus drivers might welcome Hispanic students with a "Buenos Dias," as they entered the bus in the morning; lunch menus might offer culturally appropriate foods in the students' language; and teachers might assign deaf students the opportunity to respond to questions in sign language. It was an ambitious effort to be inclusive.

There were to be no attempts at avoidance. Deadline dates for completed forms were stamped on the forms. Severe monetary penalties were to be enforced on any school that failed to meet all requirements.

The Mankato Public Schools tasked the district mentor teacher with leading the plan. When I was selected to be district mentor in 1991, the program was a significant part of my job description. I was to be responsible for mentoring new secondary teachers in the district, supervising secondary student teachers, and developing the second year of the 10-year plan.

A district wide committee was formed, comprised of both elementary and secondary staff, both volunteers and assigned. Most of them were school leaders who understood the need for the plan, had a special interest in its development, and were dedicated to its success. The group included Kathy Parish, the district's only African-American teacher, Judy Brown, the mother of an African-American son, Bev, who taught many elementary school students who were non-native-English speakers and Sandra Wood and Jane Paapas, staff members with a strong commitment to equality for all.

Our committee's first major assignment was to plan a half-day of the opening school workshop to offer teachers the opportunity to attend sessions where 17 community agencies talked about how they provided services for the groups included in the plan. Planned Parenthood, Community Assistance for Refugees and The Society for the Blind were among them. A popular local band, The Lost Walleye, played a variety of appropriate songs to fit the theme of the day during the coffee hour. Folders containing appropriate resources for the teachers were distributed, and a thousand brightly colored paper cranes, symbolizing the schools' role in providing inclusiveness for all students, hung throughout the building.

After I was selected as the district's secondary mentor and planned the inclusivity portion of the opening day workshop, a position opened for the Director of the Alternative High School. I applied and was hired to fill the position. My colleague and friend, Pat Schmidt, replaced me as the secondary mentor.

Summary of Staff Development Efforts 1978-1993

The State Department of Education, the district school board, school administrators and teachers sought solutions to the varied ailments of public schools and the societal changes that challenged educators during this fifteen year period. They also made considerable efforts and spent large amounts of money to improve the quality of education for all students.

It appeared that some of their attempts were more successful than others, but without empirical evidence, it's difficult to know for certain. To the best of my recollection, there were no scholarly studies to measure the results of mood-altering substance policies, ESL programs, or any of the other improvement efforts.

There was some administrative monitoring of classroom instruction but there were no rewards for following the Madeline Hunter plan model and no punishment for failing to. School leadership teams did practice site-based management as they met with building leaders and created educational plans. But although those plans were reviewed, their impact on student learning was not.

Outcome-based education clearly established a method to meet a set of learning requirements in all disciplines and held students accountable for them. However, the process proved unwieldy for most teachers. Refining the model by standardizing lessons offering second and third attempts at concepts proved either too time consuming or too expensive.

Inclusive education models tried to level the playing field and ensure gender equity, sensitivity to disabilities, and respect for diverse cultures. Providing this welcoming environment for targeted groups might have contributed to their sense of acceptance in the classroom resulting in greater academic success for them. But the political winds changed directions and this highly touted ten-year plan was abruptly discarded by the state.

The State Department of Education often announced "fixes" like these and blustered about the possible consequences if these plans weren't followed to the letter. The pattern of opening the door to reforms and then quickly closing it resulted in great skepticism among teachers. Educational reform efforts made many classroom teachers snicker and tell each other, "This too shall pass."

Outstanding Teachers at West High School

While there were a couple of sluggards on the staff, most of the classrooms at Mankato West High School were filled with teachers who could have been employed at any school in the country. Social studies teacher Bob Ihrig, was a master teacher, who was twice selected as Mankato Teacher of the Year. Both times he was a finalist for Minnesota Teacher of the Year. He was known throughout the state for the quality debate teams he produced. Most important were his teaching skills. He had high expectations and required his students to meet them.

Roger Wilker, who taught English, was one of the most well-rounded scholars in our community. For years he led the West Academic Decathlon Team to the nationals. His classroom often became a theater as he performed the roles of Jonathon Edwards or Mark Twain. His performances brought literature to life.

Marty Wiltgen taught humanities across the hall from me. It was an elective English class. Offering electives based on the classics for English is risky. Registration kills most such classes. Not so with humanities at West. Marty spoke with the energy of Zig Zigler, played classical music on the piano like Liberace, and had the human relations skills of Hubert Humphrey. His classes were filled with a complete cross-section of the population of students at West.

The cross country coach, Jim Bassett was a master teacher. His understanding of conditioning and adolescent psychology gave him an edge on all of our competitors. He taught his athletes to love competing and prepared them well for it. Jim taught special education. Once I referred a ninth grade boy who couldn't read to him. Jim said, "If he wants to learn to read, I can teach him. He then fulfilled this promise.

West was filled with accomplished educators who held high expectations of their students and used all the tools in their toolboxes to construct and shape students skills in their discipline. Three though, in my opinion, stood out as the best of the best.

Jack Halvorson

Jack Halvorson was proud to be a teacher at West and he practiced teaching around the clock.

His students knew exactly what they were required to learn from him. Also, they respected his wit. They were aware that practical jokes were part of his repertoire and looked forward to a few moments of lightheartedness followed by an immediate return to the lesson. Those who finished Jack's class spoke Spanish and acquired a respect for the proud history of its native speakers. Most important, he was always approachable.

He constantly sought ways to make West a better school. He attended every event, monitored every predicament, and cheered every participant. At sporting events he was the first to arrive and the last to leave as he supervised student council members who made and sold popcorn. The profit from these sales funded the student council which he oversaw. Staff members at West took Jack's omnipresence for granted.

Jack used part of the summer months to make the next years plans for improvement. After attending a summer student council leadership camp, he developed a student leadership model whose equal I never saw. He asked several teachers to lead groups of seniors at monthly meetings, where they would plan leadership activities. These students attended junior high school activities and encouraged, cheered and supported the future Westies in a manner which modeled appropriate and supportive behaviors.

I never refused a request to sponsor an activity Jack led. I would have been remiss in not doing the small part he sometimes asked of me.

Kathy Jensen

Kathy's business education classroom was a beehive of activity with Kathy the queen bee. But Kathy ensured that the honey was made to perfection. She moved quickly and quietly from student to student helping them but not solving their problems. She was the catalyst but allowed them to do their own work.

No teacher did this in a calmer, more efficient manner than Kathy. Students viewed her as a partner in their learning process and appreciated that. The entire staff at West was delighted when she was selected as Teacher of the Year.

Rod Urtel

When Rod Urtel was hired to teach choral music, we had the worst chorus in the Conference. After one year, under his leadership, we were competitive with other schools and in two years, we were with the best. Before Rod came West's choral music participation was low. His solution was to require try outs. Raising the bar for admittance led to an increase in participation. A chorus of sixteen students grew to a chorus of sixty students. Instead of finding an empty auditorium at concerts, audience members had to arrive early to get a seat. Students who had shunned chorus before, now were joyful, proud participants. River City had singers.

Support Staff

West had two buildings. When I was transferred there, the primary building accommodated nearly all of grades 9 through 12 and the superintendent's office. The annex housed auto mechanics, technical education, special education, industrial arts classes, and the curriculum director's office. It was also the central distribution site for audio-visual materials and quarters for the district maintenance crew. West teachers had immediate access to nearly all of these services.

The close proximity to this whole crew encouraged the development of relationships. Teachers, carpenters, audio-visual employees and secretaries took coffee breaks together and became friends. These friendships resulted in better service. Ardie Detjen, one of our school secretaries, and Bob Holtorf, our school carpenter, both provided these services with a smile and customized them to meet individual teacher's needs.

Bob Holtorf

The individualized instruction that was required to accomplish the goals of outcome-based education required organizational skills and specialized, easy to use filing cabinets. While some students mastered a concept on verb usage after completing the 1st lesson, others needed 4 lessons. Locating these different prepared lessons quickly became important to the success of the OBE concept.

Teachers attempting to do this needed very efficient filing systems. I met with Bob explaining my needs. He responded, "Give me some time and I'll draw up a plan. When I've finished we'll meet again and make the necessary modifications." He measured the room and sketched its arrangement. He wanted to place the new "furniture" where it would be most accessible to students.

When we met a few days later Bob's drawing of the filing cabinet was perfect. Bob was always a partner in educating our students.

Ardie Detjen

Ardie Detjen did the typing, copying, and collating for teachers at West. She examined everything before she typed it and met with the teacher to assure everything was in order. The meetings were always pleasant and Ardie often warmly recalled her learning experience as she typed.

Ardie talked freely of her life and was one of the more popular members of the staff. She had been widowed and lost a son in a dog sled accident. Many of the teachers befriended her, taking her along to casinos and other social events.

Ardie's work allowed teachers to include exercises that they may not have otherwise been typed and resulted in more preparation time and better learning opportunities for students.

Doug Johnson

Doug Johnson was hired as director of media and technology services in 1991. His role was tasked with updating our information technology system and he took it on with gusto. In this respect resembling Stalin's five year plan in Russia, there was no room for argument. During his first three years on the job all the teachers in the district were given new computers and were trained to use them. Over the next three years computer labs became available to students in all of its schools. Tight budgets and frugal leaders notwithstanding, Doug prevailed in his battle to bring the best technology to Mankato students and staff.

Memorable Students

Erin Barnett

That Erin Barnett was my boss's daughter is immaterial. She was one of the brightest, most creative, and warmest personalities

I ever taught. Every assignment was done promptly, correctly and imaginatively. Her interactions with others, in all cases, were friendly and respectful.

While doing her oral book report, Erin captivated the entire class, which is not easy with a class filled with energetic, restless 9th graders. She involved students in her explanation of the book by requiring them to be actively involved listeners. As she introduced the main character in her novel, she handed out lemon drops to the students and asked them to describe what they experienced as they tasted them. Students responded with words like "sour," "tart," and "parching." She wrote their words on the chalk board and used them to describe the life and personality of the main character in her novel. Her whole report required students to use their senses to understand the novel she was reporting on. Students applauded when Erin completed this assignment.

Although there were others with Erin's capabilities, she paired the intellect, with the winning personality of a model student.

Kirby Hanson

Kirby Hanson was a reader. His family had left Mankato when his dad lost his teaching position in the district during a staff reduction period. Kirby had loved the small town where the family had lived before returning to Mankato, and it took time for him to adjust to the larger school environment. Reading helped fill some of the void that he experienced with the move.

Kirby read serious books and enjoyed them. He'd stop after class and share his insights from some book like *Grapes of Wrath*. Sometimes he'd ask a question or express a concern about some event in the novel either before or after class. He quietly learned and grew and sought out the intellectual challenges that other students avoided.

He was also a good wrestler. His father, Russ, was a coach and Kirby met his high standards. I knew little about wrestling, but Bev and I attended many of his matches. Bev didn't see much of Kirby though. Fearful he would get hurt, she closed her eyes much of the time.

Kirby is now a teacher, father and school leader. It is a real joy when I meet him at a Christmas or Easter church service. I am proud to have played a small role in his life.

Sophat

I met Sophat while supervising students in the library. He appeared to be playing half of hide-and-seek. He was hiding but no one was seeking. He moved about carefully while studying other students. He positioned himself at the corner of the large card catalog, where he watched everything that transpired in the room.

My concern grew as he became more animated. I approached him and asked, "Are you all right? May I help you?"

His response went far beyond what I had expected. "I am Sophat from Cambodia. My parents were killed by Pol Pot. I escaped and found my way to Kowedung Camp in Thailand, where I have lived for the past three years. My sister, who also escaped ransomed government officials to bring me here, and I live with her."

The words that spilled out were difficult to understand but he went on "I hid in the tall grass as Pol Pot's army moved in front of us. They killed their captives as I lay in the weeds on a hillside just above them." As I listened I wondered if his issues had been addressed by school administrators.

During my prep hour that afternoon, I visited with Principal Barnett to share what I had learned from Sophat. He appreciated my concern but put forward little in the way of extra help to meet Sophat's needs.

That evening as I told Beverly what we had happened, we agreed there were likely few shortcuts to making his new world more comforting and that my role in his life might simply be to listen to him. While in the library, I did that.

One Sunday afternoon about two weeks after I met Sophat, Dr. Dorland, a local optometrist known for his philanthropy, interrupted the Vikings game with a phone call. After introducing himself, he got right to the point. "I understand you are familiar with a Cambodian student at West named Sophat. I would like you to meet me at his home in 15 minutes. He lives at 127 Kings Road in upper North Mankato. That's the trailer court by Arnold Implement. He and his brother-in-law, Moon, live together and they are having some family issues. I may need your help in resolving them.

Wait a minute, I thought. Not only do I not know Moon, I don't know you.

Hesitatingly, I agreed to go and support him as he established some ground rules for Sophat, his sister, and Moon.

Dr. Dorland was seated in his car outside Sophat's mobile home when I arrived. I sat with him while he explained what was going on. "I am responsible for bringing them here. Now I must help them integrate successfully into our culture. The problem seems to be Moon is not married to Sophat's sister. He is married to another woman who also lives in Mankato. He spends time with both of them. Because of this Sophat hates him. The situation has become more and more volatile. We must calm them today or it could become violent. I will take the lead in the conversation and you jump in as you see fit."

Dorland was about five foot four inches tall and one-hundred twenty pounds and I am no Atlas. He had an air of confidence, though, as he led the way into the house, introduced me and took charge. He seated us around the table, seating Moon at the opposite end from Sophat.

It soon became apparent that no love was lost between Sophat and Moon. Angry words flew across the table and suddenly things escalated. Shouting Cambodian epitaphs, Moon picked up a boom box, hurled it at Sophat's head, threw his chair back, and dived for a kitchen cabinet drawer.

Shocked, I remained seated in my chair, wishing I were home watching the Vikings. With the swiftness of a mountain lion Dorland bested Moon in a race to the drawer and firmly planted himself against it. Although his eyes showed no fear, his body seemed frail.

Without warning, he collapsed to the floor. In a raspy voice he called to Moon. "I am a very sick man," I have been good to you.

Please! Do not cause me to die." He then unbuckled his belt, pulled his slacks down to his knees and displayed a large black and blue bruise surrounding his groin. "Look!" he said to Moon.

Waving me over, he commanded in a whisper, "Get Sophat out of here immediately! He's in danger! Take him to your home. I'll bring his clothes later and we'll figure out what to do next. I'm fine. This bruise is from an angiogram that I had Thursday. Don't worry about me. I'll see you at your home."

Sophat moved in with Bev and me and quickly became part of our family. Our home was a small; quad-level with an unoccupied room in the basement. The next level up had a family room that had been converted from a single garage. It also had a laundry and half-bath. Sophat moved into the vacant bedroom and used the laundry room to dress for school.

He ate with us, worshipped with us, joined in our family games and entertainment and was held accountable for his share of the family chores. He seemed to be happy and adjusting well but he surprised us one evening when he announced he had made arrangements to move in with an older couple in the neighborhood, Bob and Dorothy Christianson. Dorothy worked as an aide in the library at West and had encouraged Sophat to make the change. They had more room, a private full bath, and financial assistance that we could not offer. At first we were stung by his decision but over time learned to accept and even appreciate it.

The Apple Gang

April 1 is a special day on the school calendar for most teachers. They arise early to mentally prepare for the coming onslaught of April Fool's Day practical jokes. Alertness and delayed response times are essential for survival. Most of those jokes from students are simple one liners like; "Did you hear that the president is being held captive by outer space aliens?"

The usual response is, "You can do better than that. You know I'm not that easy. If I were, you'd be getting an A."

But sometimes students design elaborate pranks. On April 1st, 1989, I entered my first-period class after monitoring the hallway and saw a shiny, large, red apple on my desk. Under it was a sheet of paper with a short poem scribbled on it:

> *The apple here is left for you*
> *from some who know you well.*
> *Be prepared for more mischief*
> *before the ringing of each bell.*

> *The Apple Fool Gang*

I didn't know quite what to expect, but foreshadowing is forewarning and the poem provided the foreshadowing. I was on the alert. Between first and second period class I stayed in the classroom. I feigned grading papers at my desk while surveying things carefully as students entered class. A gathering of four or five boys in the back of the room caught my attention. They were watching me and looking at something on the floor. Hmm! I thought. The April Fool's Day game is on! I moved quickly to them convinced the apple mystery was about to be solved.

No such luck. The boys were just swapping tales. Aware that I may have missed the real action while moving to the diversion, I glanced at my desk. There sat another apple on a sheet of paper.

My students shouted, "What's on your desk?"

"Just an apple," I responded.

"Read us what's on the sheet of paper," they called.

I did.

Clue 2

Too bad you didn't see us
when we sneaked into your room
but we are always tricky
in April, May and June.

For the rest of the day all my classes followed suit. At the beginning of each period I was distracted while an apple was placed on my desk. Under each apple was a poetic clue to lead me to the identities of the Apple Fool Gang. At the end of the day, I had five poems and apples and no idea who gave them to me.

In desperation I turned to the sources who always knew everything that went down at West—the secretaries. As usual, they came through. Sandy Gemlo, John Barnett's secretary, had overheard a revealing conversation.

The entire Frisch family had been involved. Robin, Jonathon, Arthur, and Jessica had all been my students. All scholars, none of them was a pushover. Sometimes they might question a test item or an assignment, but never in a vigorous way.

Once the members of the Apple Fool's Gang were identified, I had to retaliate. Finally, I decided to purchase an apple tree for them, attach an appropriate poem to it, and sneak it onto their lawn.

I asked Sandy Gemlo to obtain their address, purchased the apple tree, and wrote the poem.

The Hole Apple Truth Discovered

The apples were good.
The poems were great.
But being discovered
Was always your fate

A sleuth I'm not
now that's for sure
but other sources
have made it clear.

Now plant ths tree
and make it grow.
We'll share the fruit
again somehow.

I delivered the tree and the poem to their house. It appeared nobody was home, so I left them both on the front porch. A week passed with no response. We were together in class, passed each other in the halls, and there was no indication that anyone knew anything about the Apple Fool Gang.

Finally, I returned to Sandy Gemlo and told her what had happened. "Roger, I'm sorry. I led you astray." she said, "The Frisches have moved. They no longer live there."

After school I hurried to my van and drove to the old Frisch house. There on the front porch, right where I left it, sat the tree. I got the tree and loaded it in the van. That evening I planted the tree in the yard of my new home on Madison Lake. I then added to the poem.

The Hole Apple Story – Part 2

The mischief that was planned
with the gift of the apple tree
was truly thrown askew
with the move that was made by thee.

The tree has now been planted
on the west side of my lawn
but the fruit that it shall bear
will be saved and eaten none.

For this will be the Frisch tree
that compensates their toil
on that Apple Fool's day,
when they did prove my foil.

Still there was no reaction until the next April Fool's Day. That morning, when Bev and I were backing out of our driveway, she exclaimed, "Look at that! There are apples on our flowering crab."

When we stopped to investigate, the apples were taped to the tree with this poem:

> *The apple gang has struck again.*
> *We now know where you live.*
> *Watch out for future apple tricks,*
> *which we still plan to give.*

The Frisch tree bore no fruit that fall, so I bided my time. In the fall of 1992, we finally had a small crop of apples. I harvested them in October, and Bev and I made our first batch of apple butter. It was delicious I delivered two pints to the Frisch business in Judson. The children's father readily accepted the role of accomplice.

On April Fool's evening in 1993 our dog, Boomer, grew agitated. He went to the door barking and begging to go. Bev walked to the garage door, turned on the exterior light, and looked out the kitchen window. Two girls were running away from the house toward their car. A brown bag containing apple candies and other apple-flavored treats were left on our doorstep.

On April 1st, 1994 I was in my office as the new Principal of Alternative High School. I was holding an intake meeting with parents of a new student when I heard laughter in the outer office. I was surprised when my administrative assistant, Patsy Lang, knocked on the door and interrupted the meeting. She was holding an apple pie. She said, "Two apples just delivered this pie for you. They didn't want to talk, but if you hurry you should be able to catch them. I'll cover your meeting for you."

I ran down the two flights of stairs and through the corridors to the parking lot. As I exited the door I saw two red apples getting into an apple mobile and heading toward the parking lot exit.

When I returned to my office, Patsy said that two girls dressed in red plastic bags, filled with cotton stuffing, had delivered the pie and told her, "Tell Mr. Stoufer The Apple Fool gang has struck."

The Frisches graduated and I retired. My retirement prompted another Frisch apple attack, and I responded after the autumn apple harvest with a revised version of Robert Frost's *Mending Wall* to fit our situation.

Although the harvest was minimal, we collected the few apples there were and delivered them under the cover of dark to the Frisches, accompanied by the poem:

Apples and Such

Something there is that loves an apple joke,
that makes the soul fill with joy,
and warms the cockles of the heart,
and brings memories of April Fools past.
The time of the apple joke is another thing.
Years and years have passed and yet the apple joke continues,
To please the aging teacher—the retiree I mean.
No one has seen the apple gang—or heard them at work.
But at unexpected times we find the apples there.
I let my friends know over cups of coffee and apple cake,
And on a day we reminisce of pleasant times,
And talk of Frisches in our lives.

We eat the apple cake as we talk,
From each, different stories of Frischery are told,
and some are more exact than others.
We have to pause to laugh at tricks they did.
"Apples and riddles were on my desk each period of the day."
We wear our voices thin with laughing.
Oh, more to remember than is usual.
These Frisches. They were inventive.
They created and continued far into the future.
They are all riddles, and I am riddled.
The apples I continue to enjoy
And so I share with them.
"I have an apple tree dedicated to you."
"Fall is the time your apples are ripe."
I pick the six apples from the tree.
"Why do I not locate the apple gang
to bring them their apples?"
Before I gather their harvest I'd better locate them
To ensure the harvest is shared.
Something there is that loves that apple gang,
That appreciates its humor.
He said it to himself,
"Good apple gangs make life more pleasant."

It seemed likely that the Apple Fool Gang jokes had come to a natural end. But in 2006 when Beverly and I decided to move back to Mankato and sell our lake home, I told the buyers of our home, Mark and Nancy Weichman, "I will sell you everything but the apple tree. I can't sell that because it doesn't belong to me. It belongs to the Apple Fool Gang." Then I told them the story.

Mark and Nancy stopped me short when I said the names of the gang members. Both of them were on the faculty at Bethany College and worked with the children's mother. Delighted they agreed that the harvest from the little tree would belong to the Frisch family.

That fall Mark remembered our agreement and surprised us when he delivered the Frisch apples to our house. The gang members had spread their wings and left Mankato, making it difficult to locate them. Robin was married and the mother of two adolescent children. Jonathon had completed advanced degrees in college. Arthur had passed away. Jessica, the youngest, was teaching English in the Rochester Public Schools. After finding out where they were, Bev and I made a large apple crisp from the apples and delivered it to the Frisch parents. Of course there was a poem that accompanied it.

The Apple Joke (Continued)

Apples, apples everywhere
And not a Frisch around.
Their harvest was abundant
But they cannot be found.

Should their fruit be spoiled
because they have disappeared.
The cold might destroy it
that is the greatest fear.

A search is now required
to verify their homes.

Time has passed since we met last
and they are grown and gone.

The soil that holds their tree
has passed to other hands.
The Frisch tree was exempted
According to contractual demand.

The apple joke will continue
for at least another year.
The fruit is more than apples.
Its measure is in cheer.

When the cake pan that had held the apple crisp was left at our door it contained apple treats. The Apple Fool joke now has a twenty-one year history.

Maybe the Apple Fool's Gang has struck for the last time but maybe not.

Departing from West

Leaving West was difficult for me. I had enjoyed the camaraderie with the staff, the challenges with the students, and the opportunities to grow. I was always proud to introduce myself by announcing, "I'm Roger Stoufer. I teach English at West High School."

COMPUTER ERA

Alternative High School, Mankato, MN 1991-1995

The Alternative Adventure

My fate in schools included change
Not what I really sought.
But I'm uncertain to this day
How I became a boss.

Superintendent Beilfuss looked up as I walked by the open door of his office, waved for me to enter, and called, "Stoufer, come in here for a second. We need to talk. He lifted some folders from a chair near his desk and said, "Sit down."

I expected he had questions about the portion of the inclusiveness workshop that I had been asked to plan. As usual, he got right to the point. "Stoufer, Mark Lindquist has resigned as principal at the Alternative High School. He took a position in Saint Cloud. Do you have any interest in that job?"

My response was immediate. "No, sir. None."

"Well, let me tell you about it before you make up your mind. I hear you and your brother are partners in a used car business. My dad built racing engines for some of the best drivers in the Chicago area."

When I offered that my brother, too, had built race-car engines, he ignored me saying, "Dad had a knack for that kind of thing. He didn't like the business part as much as the mechanical stuff. That's the way lots of these alternative kids are. They need a spot where they thrive."

"I agree with that," I said. "I'm the first high school graduate in my family. My brother would have fit perfectly in an alternative program."

"At our central administrative meeting yesterday, your name was mentioned for filling Lindquist's position. Think about it and let me know if you're interested."

With that he stood, dismissing me.

Bev and I were working at the central administrative offices together that day making copies of the program for the inclusiveness workshop. When I left Beilfuss's office I pulled her aside and said quietly, "Beilfuss just offered me the Alternative High School principal's position, and I've never even been in the place." We both laughed.

The next few days were filled with preparations for the workshop. We typed and made copies of the program and completed all the details necessary for teachers to choose appropriately from the menu of offerings. Driven by our time schedule, there was little time for me to think about Beilfuss's proposal.

Later I made some calls and talked with friends about the position. After receiving some encouragement from them, I decided to apply but leave the door open to rejecting the position if it was officially offered. The mentor position I was already slated to fill excited me, but I was also intrigued by the thought of leading program designed to meet the needs of at-risk kids.

After I applied, I was one of four applicants scheduled for an interview. It was then that Boyd Schuler, a good friend and president of the local teacher's union called and shared with me that there were problems at Alternative. The staff, comprising 6 full time and 11 half time positions, was deeply divided because of a sexual discrimination complaint the previous year. Boyd suggested I ask Gordon Gibbs, the district personnel director, for a copy of the report detailing this before accepting the position. When I read the report it confirmed what Boyd had told me. Naïvely, I was confident this would not be a major problem for me and I moved forward with my plan to pursue the position.

My interview—with alternative teachers Jean Jackson and Ann Long; school secretary Patsy Lang; Alternative student, Jay Michels and Gordon Gibbs seemed to go well. My responses, for the most part, went unchallenged, and their demeanor seemed encouraging. These thoughts were affirmed the following day when I was offered the position. I responded that I would need three days and I would give them my answer on Monday.

Sunday night I told Bev, "I've decided not to take the position. I've been looking forward to being the district mentor for a full year. I'm not going to give that up. The choice for me is whether to spend the next year working with at-risk kids or aspiring teachers. It seemed as if the choice was at two ends of the spectrum: Those seeking success in education and those avoiding it.

The next morning I woke at 6:00 and changed my mind again. Restlessly, I reviewed the pros and cons of the decision. The pros for alternative seemed stronger. It offers me the opportunity to use my counseling training; I might continue working on what I started with students who struggled with substance abuse; I will learn what it's like to lead a staff; I might pay back the debt I owe to Pastor A.E. Norsan, Mrs. Olson, and all the people who encouraged me during my adolescence; and most importantly, I might help some young people find their way to a fulfilling life.

I was convinced that the counseling training I had received from my former academic advisor, Jack Auger had equipped me with strategies that could prove effective, and that the job offered me the opportunity to test those skills. I wanted that challenge. At 53 I knew this opportunity would not come again. I explained my reasoning with Bev, and she agreed. I called Beilfuss and informed him of my decision. He thanked me and arranged for me to meet with Assistant Superintendent Dave Dakken.

I liked and trusted Dave. I told him, "Dave, if after one year I don't wish to do this again, I want your acceptance, just as I will accept it if you decide you'd like me to return to West.

Dave reached for my hand, shook it hard, and said, "Deal!"

Alternative's History and Culture

The first thing I did was to review Alternative's student handbook, the roster, and the district's policies for the school. The roster showed that 120 students ages 16 to 19 were registered or planning to register. While 24 credits were needed to graduate, students enrolled had earned from 6 to 22. There were more girls than boys and some were students from West, whom I had known to be difficult.

Alternative was already in violation of some district policies. Its students were allowed supervised smoke breaks in a designated area on the grounds. The rationale was clear—many of the students placed a higher value on smoking than on a high school diploma. If they couldn't smoke, they would quit school.

Teachers and students were on a first-name basis. Credits were awarded quarterly rather than annually. There was no effort to differentiate between excused and unexcused absences; seven absences from a class resulted in an automatic dismissal from class.

While reviewing the district's spread sheets for workshop meetings with my new staff, I discovered that the allocated compensatory funding wasn't being spent. Compensatory funding was additional per-pupil funding based on free or reduced-lunch status. Because textbooks, equipment, and supplies seemed sparse and antiquated, that funding became an agenda item for our meeting.

Other agenda items included staff meetings, student appointments, staff evaluation procedures, addressing student concerns, and protocol for staff and students reporting problems to me. When the agenda was completed, I said to my secretary Patsy Lang, "I want to make copies of this. Where's our copy machine?"

She replied, "We don't have one of our own. We share with Community Education. We're allowed to use it from 1:00 until 2:30 p.m."

I immediately called the business director, Ed Waltman. His initial response to my request for a copier was, "No!" But after some back and forth, he found a used copy machine for us and it was installed the next day. I felt like a kid in a candy store who had been given a huge Butterfinger. This was a small victory, but it won me respect from the staff.

At the first staff meeting, I announced that I would like to meet all 120 students individually. The staff agreed that it was a good idea and Patsy scheduled the 120 appointments. This proved to be a wonderful opportunity for me to gain a full appreciation of the student's varying circumstances.

The genesis of the Alternative High School was the teenage parenting program. Carolyn Nafstead, with friends Sylvia McCarty, Joyce Burgess and Pat Peterson had founded it. Twenty of our girls enrolled in Alternative High School classes were teen mothers. The teen age parenting program (TAPP) led still by Carolyn Nafstead, taught health tips for pregnancy, child care, and family planning. We offered child care through a nursery managed by Jean Jackson. She and

Carolyn used it as a laboratory to give students supervised practice at caring for their babies. They also discussed child-care problems and helped the young mothers find solutions to them. Questions like "My baby had a loose stool last night and spent much of the evening crying. Should I have taken her to the emergency room?" were analyzed.

The TAPP teachers dedicated themselves to preventing their students from becoming pregnant again. Working together with Planned Parenthood, they followed a curriculum that explained the increasing difficulties that single mothers faced with each additional child, along with the social and financial changes. Avoiding sermons and sticking to the facts, Jean and Carolyn believed there efforts had some positive result in persuading our girls to be cautious.

Research has shown that a large percentage of adolescent girls engage in sexual behavior to please or keep a boyfriend. They are, as the song goes, *"Seeking Love in all the Wrong Places."* They experience little or no pleasure in the sex act. Research indicates that their family experience frequently is the leading cause of their adolescent sexual encounters.

Quite often the young mothers viewed their babies as objects that would provide them with a permanent loving relationship. TAPP teachers tried to get them to abandon their misconceptions and forced them to recognize the realities of their situation. These realities were based in the duty they had accepted in deciding to raise their own children.

I met all of the TAPP students first, and conversations between us flowed easily. Kayla told me that she lived with her parents and four siblings in a double-wide trailer.

"Do you all leave for school or work in the morning?" I asked. "Isn't it hectic?"

"We have to hurry," she said. "We don't fiddle around combing our hair too long."

I avoided asking intrusive questions and tried to listen more, talk less, and avoid being judgmental. Nearly all of the students shared their stories and future plans freely. April, a TAPP girl from a neighboring community, was planning to be married after graduation; Angie, who had attended the Rudy Perpich Fine Arts School, looked forward to opening her own tattoo parlor; Mike was going to work for his dad on their hog farm.

When I asked what had happened at East or West, the most frequent response was they had skipped too many classes, or I heard "The assistant principal hated me," or "I didn't like the kids there. This is better." When pushed, most of the kids accepted responsibility for their own choices.

Jane Schuck, the principal at Dakota Meadows Middle School, and Sharon Fitch, the principal at both Jefferson and Eagle Lake Elementary, interrupted my schedule and encouraged me to examine the differing roles of an area learning center and an alternative high school. They both believed redesigning our school to an area learning center would provide greater opportunities to assist more at-risk students. They explained why, and referred me to other sources.

In the evenings I found time to consider their proposal. Making the change seemed simple enough. It required applying to the Minnesota Department of Education and accepting the added responsibilities that were required of an area learning center. These included:

1. Providing a summer school program for all qualifying at-risk students in the area.

2. Providing a middle-level program for area children ages 12-16.

3. Providing after-school educational opportunities for students.

After brief consideration I met with Jane, Sharon, Dave Dakken and Gene Johnson of the department of education. Upon learning that there were ways to help 12-16 year olds who were at risk, Dave Dakken was interested. After hearing Gene stumble through a very confusing explanation of additional funding, offered by an ALC designation, Dave decided to go for it.

I was charged with making it happen.

Weaving Through the Maze

Among other more minor problems that hindered the development of an ALC middle school was a fight that broke out during a P.E. class. The police had to be called. The boy who started the fight became angry when a ball hit him in the face while playing dodgeball.

He refused to comply with police requests to "assume the position" and was forcibly taken from the building to the county jail.

My only other experience with visiting a prisoner was during my early adolescence while working for Green Giant in Glencoe. A couple of my pals had "borrowed" some chrome awnings from a junked Buick one night. They were caught and jailed for 10 days until the sheriff returned from vacation. The jail was an old house with some barred cells in the basement. It was not nearly as modern or secure as the one in Mayberry that Barney Fife guarded. There was easy access to their cells, so several of us visited them, brought treats, and left a mess.

The jail in Mankato where I visited my student was far more secure and threatening. The elevator that took me from the first to the second floor was walled with bars and locked immediately upon my entrance. A guard freed me when the elevator door opened. He then secured me in the prison visiting area, which had chrome chairs anchored to the floor with half-inch bolts. There were some books, but no other furniture.

The student looked defiant when the guard brought him in. "Are you all right?" I asked.

"Hell no!" he said angrily. "The cops beat me up and I didn't do anything. I just refused to go with them."

When I suggested that might have been a mistake, he said, "I'd do it the same way again. They didn't have the right to take me to jail."

I could see this conversation was going nowhere so I said, "I'm going to call your parents when I leave. Is there anything I should tell them?"

"Keep your nose out of it. The cops have already called."

I knew his family and they were good people. I had hoped to be able to tell them that their son was remorseful. Not being a good liar, that was impossible. I did, however, call them and share what had happened. I also scheduled an appointment for them to examine how to best meet their son's future educational needs outside of school. I was convinced that many of our students were too vulnerable to tolerate his volatile personality.

Soon after that happened my student interviews concluded. The next steps were to develop a plan to familiarize myself with the curriculum being taught, establish a weekly schedule, and determine the most pressing needs of the school. Everything of course was affected by the crisis that arose daily.

One of those I created myself. Since I was not a certified administrator, my boss, Dave Dakken, was registered with the state as the school's Principal. He and I agreed to meet monthly the first year of my service to review my concerns and progress.

I was nearly late for our first scheduled meeting. I was forced to leave the building at the last minute, and out of breath from running down the stairs, I reached into my pocket for my keys, but they weren't there. They were locked in my truck. I raced to the schools day care center next door, got a clothes hanger, and tried but failed to get into the truck. I ran back inside and up the stairs. Entirely breathless by this time, I sputtered, "Patsy, call a locksmith! I've locked my keys in my truck and tell him I'm running late. I needed him 10 minutes ago."

"Roger, I think Jay, one of our students, might be able to help you. Let me give him, a call," she said.

When Jay arrived, he told me, "Roger, Usually I just use a big rock through the passenger's window to get in. I don't suppose you'd like that." He laughed loudly and said,, "I'm just putting you on." Spying that my truck had a sliding back window, he opened it with an illegal knife he carried in his pocket, reached through the opening and grabbed the keys. I got to my appointment just in the nick of time.

The next and far more serious crisis was when two female students got into a fist fight during our morning break. Afterward, I met with the girls individually and was comfortable the problem was resolved.

That was a costly error. Just before noon a student told me that each girl had arranged to have family and friends meet at the school, where all of them would settle their differences Hatfield-McCoy style.

Patsy called the police, but by the time they arrived, many of our "guests" were already there and the war had begun. The staff stepped up to the plate and hit a home run. Social Studies teacher, Kris McGuire, only five feet tall, leaped in front of a girl twice her size and prevented her from joining the fight. Dan Toegel the new World Area Studies teacher, placed one of the trespassers in the hold and moved him toward the door. Everywhere teachers were preventing the fight from spreading. I warned the other students, "If you became involved in this, your status as a student will be in jeopardy." By the time the police arrived, the riot was nearly quelled.

I called Dave Dakken to tell him what had happened and suggested that we suspend the two girls for the rest of the year. Because state law didn't allow a suspension of that duration, we informed the girls they could return as students at East for the rest of the year but they were expelled as students at Alternative. Patsy called the parents and scheduled a meeting with them.

Each of the girl's parents blamed the other girl and demanded that their daughter be allowed to continue at Alternative. When I said that was out of the question, one of the fathers glared angrily at me and said, "I'm about ready to put a real hurt on you."

I looked him in the eye and replied with my standard line when threatened "You'd pay a big price if that happened. For your sake I think you'd better leave." I felt a deep sense of relief when he had slammed the door behind him. I thought, "What in the hell am I doing here? I left a wonderful job at West for this?"

The most serious threat that I ever encountered came from a boy who was in a gang and had been in a fight at Alternative. The fight had not been on school grounds but he threatened several students at our school who were members of a different gang. I met him in my office and told him he was no longer a student here.

He replied, "You are showing me disrespect. I killed a guy in Minneapolis for doing that."

Although it was unnerving, I did not allow him to see it. I knew that was what he wanted.

"I'm not worried about that, I said to him. You're so full of anger and hate that tomorrow you'll hate someone else more than me. Let's go downstairs and get you signed up for the GED program and then I'll give you a ride home."

I never saw him again after that day.

The girl's fight, the threat, and our response to it became the hot topic for discussion at our staff meetings and in the faculty lounge. The staff made an effort to analyze our responses to situations like these and to determine if there were ways we could improve on them. Klea Brewton Fitzgerald, a social studies teacher, attended a workshop that examined conflict resolution programs being used in Minnesota schools. She liked what she heard of the program being used at Patrick Henry High School in Minneapolis and approached me with a proposal to implement it in our school.

Klea studied school conflict resolution programs being used nationally, and together we reviewed staff surveys and student council contributions. We decided to use the Patrick Henry model and prepared to train counselors. We moved full speed ahead to complete the plans for a program that would reduce the conflict in our school. Klea sought volunteer student counselors and drafted other students who were fit for it. When this was accomplished, she asked careers teacher, Paulette Ford, to assist her with the program. Together they created the following model:

1. Students involved in conflict could request a resolution meeting. Request forms would be obtained from Klea or Paulette. They must include a summary of the conflict.

2. Students involved in the conflict must both agree to arbitration.

3. Student counselors would be selected by Klea/Paulette.

4. Student counselors would be given a summary of the conflict.

5. Student counselors would determine the time and place for the resolution but Klea or Paulette would approve the site.

6. Afterward, a summary of the results would be given to Klea and me.

7. All counselors had to be trained and approved by a certified training group before being assigned.

Under Klea's leadership the program reduced interventions that required my presence by fifty percent over the next year. The next year I submitted a nomination to the State Department of Education to honor Klea for her work. She was recognized that spring for developing the most innovative new alternative high school program in Minnesota.

The Development of the Middle (Model) School

After our first meeting to review my progress as a principal, Dave Dakken asked me to take a seat with him on the community-based Anti-Violence Committee. The committee was tasked with creating a plan to reduce youth crime in our community. On it were:

1. Mankato Public Safety Director – Glen Gabriel

2. North Mankato Police Chief – Les Ennis

3. Blue Earth County Attorney – Ross Arneson

4. Blue Earth County Lead Corrections Officer – Jerry Haley

5. Nicollet County Lead Corrections Officer – Steve Kley

6. Blue Earth County Assistant Human Services Director – Floyd

7. Nicollet County Assistant Human Services Director – Sue Serbuss

8. Mankato police officer – Charles Reasnor

9. North Mankato Deputy Police Chief – Mike Pulis

10. Assistant Superintendent of Schools – Dave Dakken

11. Alternative High School Director – Roger Stoufer

At the first meeting I attended, Dave asked me to explain how the school's new alternative learning center status allowed us to develop a middle school program for at-risk kids. When I was halfway through my explanation, Gabriel, a burly Florida native with a loud voice interrupted me saying, "I nominate this guy to chair a sub-committee to develop a plan to use this new school as an early intervention model designed to reduce street crimes committed by adolescents. If we can keep these young kids off the street, we'll have a better chance of keeping them from hooking up with the older thugs that will use them."

Just like that, Floyd, Sue, Steve, and I became the new committee. Gabriel was not on the committee, but it was clear he would provide input.

After several subcommittee meetings, we met with the committee to announce the following model that we had developed.

1. This program would meet the needs of chronically truant 12-16 year old students with behavioral problems. Its primary goal was to help them develop the skills required to succeed in their home schools using measurable standards and a clear process.

2. The program would have two teachers and accommodate fifteen students.

3. The student application process would include a contractual agreement requiring parental cooperation. This agreement would include rules for attendance and behavioral guidelines. Parents and all involved agencies were to be represented at monthly board meetings to review issues of concern.

4. Transportation to the site would be provided by the district.

5. Curriculum and texts would provided by the home school. Reading, writing, arithmetic and coping skills were the primary curricular focus.

6. Policies and guidelines that developed would require unanimous agreement of all the agencies represented on the anti-violence task force.

7. Funding was to be shared by all of the agencies involved.

The devil is always in the details and those weren't up to our committee. They were to be debated first in the anti-violence committee and then among each of the agencies involved.

After our presentation Public Safety Director Gabriel immediately became an advocate for the plan.

Jerry Haley, professorial as always, asked the first question. "Where are you housing this classroom filled with miscreants?"

"I want it," Gabriel said immediately. "The entire lower level of the law enforcement center is vacant. We'll furnish it and it can become a school. Hell, if they get out of line, I've got a gun."

There followed a discussion of the appropriateness of using the law enforcement as a school for truants. When a committee member disagreed too strongly with Gabriel, he again reminded them he carried a gun, making the group break out into laughter.

The committee finally agreed that if we proceeded on this endeavor, the law enforcement center would be considered as a site. The first hurdle had been jumped.

At the next meeting, Dave Dakken questioned how we could get the truants to attend a new school any better than the old one. Gabriel replied, "Call me. I'll send a squad and two cops to pick them up. We won't need to do that very often before they catch on." Again we discussed the possibility and decided to take him up on the offer. By the meeting's conclusion I agreed to ride with the police, if it was necessary, to pick up a truant. We now had a site and we were committed to getting students to it.

Next came the highest hurdle of all, funding. Dave Dakken said, "Roger can frame a letter to send to agency heads describing our model and setting a meeting date to discuss and approve the funding."

The rationale for shared funding was based on the assumption it would save money for all of them. Sending students to correctional programs outside the community was expensive.

Dakken asked me to preside at the meeting of the agency heads. The discussion of the school went well until the funding issue arose. At that point the head of Nicollet County Human Services glared at Dakken and snarled, "It appears District 77 is once again shirking its duties and trying to dump its responsibilities onto human services."

Dakken shot back, "That's about the most inane comment I've heard from anyone in all my years in this business."

Jerry Haley quickly intervened. "Cliff," he said. "If I can convince you that this school will actually reduce Nicollet County's expenditures on adolescent placement, will you agree to share in the program's costs?"

"I'll listen, but I'm not making any promises."

Haley presented the numbers and the meeting dragged on. Finally, Cliff agreed to participate.

We submitted a job description to the district's personnel director, Gordon Gibbs and opened a nationwide search for candidates. It was more than a little disappointing when, after two weeks, we had received only five applications. Nobody wanted the damn job! Spending eight hours a day locked up in the basement of a law enforcement center with 15 incorrigible 12-to-16 year olds must not have seemed appealing. We re-wrote the description, emphasizing that "candidates will have the opportunity to assist in developing a cutting-edge, interagency, at-risk youth intervention model." The school took its name from the job description and became the Model School.

The revised description fooled nobody. High unemployment notwithstanding, we found few takers. We decided to select from our minuscule pool of candidates.

Bev Berger was a local mother of three. Her children had been my students at West. Even though she had no experience, the interview team consisting of Gabriel, Haley, Serbuss and I were all convinced she was perfect for the job.

Wayne had an impressive resume. He had worked in similar

programs and written grants to fund them through private philanthropic sources. The interview, though, went poorly. He described several negative school experiences and his failures to achieve some of his work goals. Gabriel finally interrupted him saying, "My God! I don't know if I want to be in the same room with you. The ceiling might collapse." But eager to proceed, we offered both Wayne and Bev the jobs.

I was tasked with selecting qualified Model School students from the list of applicants, interviewing parents, procuring their signature on our parental cooperation contract and arranging transportation.

School principals had submitted applications for 22 candidates. Two were from Lake Crystal. The superintendent there was familiar with ALC laws, and knew we were required to serve students outside the district. He was displeased when I didn't select his students. "I was confident that they weren't as well suited as the ones I had chosen to fill the 15 slots.

To say the least we got off to a rocky start. In our planning we had failed to provide a "duty free lunch hour" and a preparation period; deciding instead to let the teachers work that out. When it became clear that a single teacher could not control the gang of 15, the anti-violence committee members agreed to relieve them for lunch. Supervisors took their turn and brought their talents. West Assistant Principal, Tom Brekke, an accomplished juggler, taught the students to juggle, Gabriel sat them in a circle and told cop stories and I taught how movies were made.

That mistake forced all of us on the committee to develop a clear understanding of the culture we were dealing with. That, in turn, improved our planning.

Nevertheless, it soon became obvious that without adjustments the program was doomed to failure. A staffing change was made and an aide added. Bev became the lead teacher and dedicated her heart and soul to making the program succeed. She enlisted the aid of police officers, community volunteers, and Americorps participants. Under her leadership students were surrounded by nurturing professionals. The local newspaper publicized the school and community support grew.

The next curricular improvement was offering a woodworking class. That was to be a tougher nut to crack, and required the use of all the tools in my toolbox.

Tom Anderson, the Director of Community Education, was in charge of the Lincoln building. The alternative school was like a tenant who used the third floor for the school, a room on first floor for daycare, and a share of the parking lot. Even though part of the sublevel at Lincoln was a modern wood shop that was vacant, Tom had made it clear that this space was not available for us. He had no trust we could manage the students with the resources we had.

Police liaison officers Marcus Erickson and Chris Boyer worked closely with both the Model School and our senior high program. Both of them recognized that keeping at-risk students in school required more carrots than sticks and they were always planting ideas in my mind.

One that offered potential to become a huge carrot was the opportunity for Model School students to earn a trip to Boundary Waters Canoe Area. Points were awarded based on academic performance, attendance, behavior, and initiative. Thermometers for each student were placed on the classroom wall to keep them apprised of their progress.

Marcus had built a wooden canoe for himself and wanted to help the model school students build their own for the Boundary Waters trip. Because the shop was supposedly available to community members, he suggested we take the initiative and clean and reorganize it. He would then ask to use it after school.

I approved this without consulting Tom, hoping that the improved shop would please him. That was a huge miscalculation.

Tom called me at 5:00 p.m. that afternoon and asked, "Who the hell rearranged the shop? Did you approve this?" Without offering me an opportunity to respond he said, "Meet me in the shop, now!"

My mind raced with explanations as I went reluctantly downstairs. When I entered the shop he glared at me as he growled, "I think this was that cop Erickson's idea. Was it?"

"No, Tom. I'm completely responsible for this. We've talked several times about our school's need to add woodworking to our curriculum. I hoped our clean-up might lead to your acceptance."

"Clean-up! Hell! You just rearranged the place. I'm having all I can do to keep myself under control."

"That would be bad for both of us Tom," I said.

He looked at me and stepped quickly away. I headed back up the stairs to get my coat and lock the office door. When I got there the phone was ringing. "I'd like to come up and apologize," Tom said.

"Not tonight, Tom. Let's both think this over a bit before we review it." I still didn't trust his ability to control his anger and believed another day might settle both of us down.

The next morning when I arrived, Tom was in my outer office talking to Patsy. He apologized and we decided to develop a plan for the location of the tools and how to safely instruct the students. I would regularly observe the instructor that taught the shop class and Marcus and Chris would work with the Boundary Waters group building their canoe. This was the beginning of a stronger partnership between Tom and me. We met regularly and never mentioned this incident again. Together, we worked through the normal conflicts that exist in a shared building.

Marcus and Chris, with the help of some students and some of our funding, built the canoe and chaperoned the Boundary Waters trip. Johnson Reel, and other local businesses, provided fishing equipment, and camping supplies. When the students got home, they whined about the mosquitoes and the hard work like all teenagers.

The *Free Press* stories about the school increased the public's awareness. A retired science professor from Minnesota State volunteered to help the teachers develop a science program, Hilltop Kiwanis helped fund the day care program and Lions and The Centenary United Methodist Church awarded us a cash scholarship.

The publicity also helped the Alternative High School. Several current and former faculty members from the University including former education professor Bob Utermohlen and former math professor Virginia Christian volunteered to serve as tutors and mentors. They provided important individualized instruction and became strong partners in our effort to help our kids succeed.

The need for more funding for our programs drove me to constantly seek new sources. Although obtaining special grant funding for our programs from the state legislature was a long shot, John Dorn, our local representative, was able to obtain a committee hearing for our funding proposal. Marcus, school psychologist Ginny Nimmo, a parent and I were invited to testify. The presentations of Marcus and the parent were particularly convincing. We were awarded $50,000 to develop more innovative programming.

Despite all of our efforts, we were unable to provide the necessary curriculum. We lacked the resources to develop strong, individualized math and reading programs. Jostens offered a full reading and math computer based curriculum but they required the purchase of both the hardware and the software. Today my nieces and nephews routinely use programs like the Jostens program we couldn't afford.

Special Assistance for High Risk Students

I held weekly meetings for high school students who we determined needed special help. These were predicated upon staff referrals. I sometimes received notes like this one from the teachers:

Roger,

Yesterday in American literature we were reading from Sylvia Plath's, *The Bell Jar*. When the topic of suicide was discussed, Maria blurted out, "That's what I should do. That would solve my problem." I am concerned and would like to attend the SAT meeting to examine the possibility of an intervention.

   Kathleen

   The Student Assistance Team, consisting of the Blue Earth County chemical dependency counselor assigned to Alternative, school psychologist, Ginny Nimmo, school counselor, Ruth Ariens, the teacher who had made the student referral, and I gathered every Wednesday in my office. We designed interventions and arranged for follow-up reports and monitored the progress of ongoing interventions. At every meeting, we discussed 10 to 15 cases from possible dropouts to victims of domestic abuse.

   One such victim was Maria. She had moved with her boyfriend from Denver to Mankato and he had become increasingly controlling, forcefully restraining her and telling her who she could socialize with and when. Eventually, she had to report everything she did to him.

   Fearing for her safety, we decided to help Maria return to her parents in Colorado. Our SAT team (Student Assistance Team) decided to assist her in leaving him. Because funds were lacking and district administration would have rejected the plan, we moved with stealth and speed to get her to safety. Together, we bought Maria a bus ticket and helped her leave town while her boyfriend was at work, ensuring that she couldn't be followed. On her way out, she stopped in my office for a hug and thanked everyone for their help. Like so many other students we helped, we remained uncertain of the final results, but were confident we had made a sound decision. Now it was up to her to learn from her experience. We never heard from her again.

When I became principal, I changed the procedure for the SAT team. Previously, matters were discussed at a Friday, noon-hour staff meeting, which I believed violated student confidentiality. I began requiring written concerns and limited the number of people with access to the information. At first this drew objections. One teacher left me a letter saying, "Many of our students are or can be dangerous. It is your responsibility to allow a free flow of information to the entire staff. Without it we can't protect ourselves from them."

When I met with her, I reviewed the applicable privacy laws and told her that Dave Dakken had supported the changes I had made. I also told her that her letter to me would go into her permanent file, and I advised her not to communicate with me in that manner again because letters left a permanent record of incriminating evidence.

Some of our SAT referrals were as simple as students underperforming in the classroom. One such situation involved a student referred from West, primarily due to failing grades. These failures occurred in spite of the fact the student's IQ hovered around one-hundred-forty. At mid-term, with us, he was again failing all of his classes. Several of his teachers referred him to the team. Thinking outside the box, our school counselor, Ruth Ariens, suggested we send him to college using the Post-Secondary-Enrollment-Options-

Program. Under this program, the state paid all expenses for the student to earn high school credits at college. Dave Ruthenbeck, a former neighbor of mine, was a counselor at Mankato State. I secured his approval, and we registered the student binding him with a contract that required him to attend every class and earn a B average. The student maintained a 3.5 GPA at the University.

Building Parent Partnerships

Decisions as important as the post-secondary options plan always required parental input. Improving that element was vital to the school's success. Rod, a careers teacher, had a parent organization at Alternative when I came on board. I was disappointed when only four parents came to his September parent-teacher meeting. Although the numbers were small, the meeting demonstrated potential for a meaningful partnership between teachers and parents. I thought about ideas to work on this and called a staff meeting to gather input. Although Rod was controversial and seen as difficult by some staff members, I hoped they would work with us to develop a stronger parent.

At the meeting I volunteered to call the parents and personally invite them to the October meeting. When I called them, I told them the agenda, which included planning social events—the Halloween and Christmas parties, a spring picnic and a graduation party in May. Knowing how strongly they desired their children to graduate, I hoped this would be an incentive for them to come. It was. Twenty-five parents and five teachers came to the October meeting, where we shared coffee and cookies, and formed a committee to plan the spring graduation party.

The committee's primary goal was to get a share of the community funding used for graduation parties at East and West. Those schools were willing partners but required our student's parents to assist in the soliciting of contributions from local merchants for gifts to be distributed through a drawing at the party. Two of our mothers offered to lead this project and along with administrative assistant, Patsy Lang and Jean Jackson, they organized and implemented a memorable party for our graduates the following spring.

These parents were solid, regular folks. We spent virtually no time trying to determine what had caused their kids to become at-risk students. We worked together from where they were now, and hoped to remove their at risk status before they left high school.

Vocational Curriculum

Our curriculum, besides including all the required courses for graduation, also offered electives that focused on vocational skills. Two of our full-time teachers, Rod Olson and Paulette Ford, taught courses designed to develop workplace skills and help students find their niche in the work world. They helped students find employment, monitored their workplace progress, and gave them academic credit for success at work.

To be successful in their jobs, students were required to develop a trusting relationship with their employers. Doug Jurgens, the owner of the Champlin car wash, employed a number of our students. He knew that some of our students might need close supervision, but he was willing to take that risk.

In the spring of each year Paulette held a careers day and asked local business owners, like Doug, to meet with seniors and explain their work requirements. Over 80 percent of our qualified students were employed.

Summer School

To maintain our status as an Area Learning Center, we were required, by the State Department of Education, to offer summer school. Our first year as an ALC we did not meet this requirement. Our building was experiencing construction and with that impediment, I did not comply. I probably thought I could "get by with this" because the Department of Education appeared to be so disorganized. Earlier in the year they had set a date for reviewing our special education program and I had asked our special education teacher, Ann Long to have the paperwork in order. Ann complied, but no one showed up.

In September, Gene Johnson called from the Department of Education. He had noticed our paperwork on summer school enrollments had not been submitted. His remarks to me were caustic. However, he did simmer down when I explained the circumstances surrounding our decision.

In retrospect he had every right to be upset. Summer school was critical component for at-risk kids. It gave them an opportunity to catch up on credits and for many seniors behind in credits, it allowed them to graduate and move on with their lives.

In addition to our Alternative enrollees, students who failed a class or were behind in credits at East, West or Dakota Meadows could catch-up on credits at our summer school. We based our class offerings on this. Because we had a high number of students who had failed biology, we offered two sections of it. In this respect our area learning center designation provided us with the opportunity to reach out to meet the broader needs of our at-risk community.

The Graduation Rule

The Minnesota Department of Education was baffling. Sometimes it was encouraging, while others it seemed belittling. I guess it was the government's version of the carrot and the stick.

In 1992 the Legislature enacted a "rigorous, results-oriented" high school graduation rule for the state's public schools. It granted four years of preparation before implementing the rule and helped schools prepare before the rule applied. Satisfactory scores in reading and math had to be achieved by all students in the 1996-97 school year to fulfill the implementation of the first stage of the rule. The writing requirement took effect in the 1997-98 school year. These tests were to be administered at the eighth and eleventh grade levels. Students who achieved unsatisfactory scores were to be given additional instruction and could not graduate until their scores were satisfactory.

Enacted at the same time, was The Profile of Learning law, which, according to the statute was intended to:

1. "Measure student performance using performance based assessments compiled over time that integrate higher academic standards and higher order thinking skills and

2. include a broad range of academic experience and accomplishment necessary to achieve the goal of preparing students to function effectively as purposeful thinkers, effective communicators, self-directed learners, productive group participants and responsible citizens."

Included were ten broadly defined learning areas:

1. Read, view and listen

2. Write and speak

3. Literature and the arts

4. Mathematical application

5. Inquiry

6. Scientific applications

7. People and cultures

8. Decision making

9. Resource management

10. World languages (optional)

These ten broadly defined learning areas were beefed up with 48 high school content standards. Students were required to complete 24 content standards to graduate. Graduation requirements were as follows:

1. Complete one content standard within each group.

2. Complete two standards within learning area 6.

3. Complete at least 21 of 47 standards in learning areas 1 to 9.

4. Complete at least three other standards as electives.

5. Use computer technology in completing a required content standard in learning areas 2, 4, 5, and 6.

The school districts decided how to provide instruction under the law, including developing curricula and assessments. Students also had to demonstrate proficiency in an approved rule. The state funding to accomplish this was only $52.00 per student.

The entire alternative staff was concerned about the consequences the profile and performance based requirements might have on our at-risk population. Most of our students had dropped out of school once already. They had entered our school believing we were different. Our staff was more encouraging, more holistic, and more flexible. It seemed that the new law was a one size fits all. To better understand its impact, we invited a trainer from the State Department to enlighten us.

He began by saying, "I have spent the past 20 years in the classroom in Owatonna. I understand your concerns, but I believe they will be erased as easily as a math problem on the chalkboard as your understanding of the rule grows."

He then went on: "One of the greatest strengths of the profiles is that they are interdisciplinary. They are seamless. Don't assume the profile requirement number one of reading, listening and viewing will be taught by an English teacher. If the technical education instructors submit the most thorough bid or application to accomplish this profile, it will be awarded to them."

Confused and frustrated by the bureaucratic mess that would arise from this method of implementation, I asked, "Are you saying all ten areas identified for the content standards are to be bid out to all disciplines? "Who will determine the winning bid and based on what criteria?"

"That will be your job," he said. "You're the administrator."

"Let me get this straight," I said. "You are telling us teachers will need to write and submit proposals or bids for all the content standards they wish to teach. Teacher training and certification will not be the determining factor in assigning responsibility for fulfilling the assignment of the content standards."

"Correct."

"What happens if we refuse to comply with this?"

His face reddened, "Refusal to comply with assigning the content standards will result in loss of funding for your program."

I stopped listening and started thinking what I would say to Dave Dakken. The next day, when I told him what had been said, he laughed and answered, "That's not how we are going to assign content standards. We will assign them to appropriate disciplines, where they will be developed and written into the curriculum by professionals trained in the discipline where they fit."

When I retired in 1997 implementation of the content standards was still incomplete. The district had hired, Jane Schostag, one of my fellow English instructors at West, as full time graduation-rule coordinator. She performed admirably in a difficult position. While most teachers accepted her help, some believed her position added to the already considerable training and administrative costs of the rule.

During the last four years of my career I had to plan each day and activity more carefully, monitor and adjust to changing circumstances more frequently and review my decisions more closely than I ever had before.

In 1965 while I was negotiating with school board chairman Klammer, he told me, "You are becoming too expensive. We think of Stewart as a training ground for young teachers, and we believe you have now been trained." As my teaching career came to an end, I knew he was badly mistaken. I was still learning and being trained.

The most critical skills required of me at Alternative were the following:

Clarification Skills

Students, and sometimes parents, liked to use my words against me. Often I had to ask "is that clear?" During student intakes I explained that the seventh absence from any class caused a fail for the quarter. After reviewing that statement from the student handbook I always asked "Is that clear?"

I also learned to record all student infractions in writing and have students and parents sign the dated documents stating the consequences for the infraction. For example, the contract signed by parents of students entering the Model School read, "I will support the decisions the staff makes to maintain control of my child's attendance and behavior."

Because some parents regularly sided with their children regarding school officials' decisions, I made a contract with them that required their support. If parents violated the contract, the student would be returned to the home school of East, West or Dakota Meadows.

One student regularly became "sick" during the school day. Teachers gave her a place to rest but refused her request to go home. Once, she secretly called her father and begged him to rescue her. "Please, Daddy! I'm so sick and they won't listen to me. Just come down in the basement at the law enforcement center and get me during lunch hour. Please!" He agreed and we dismissed her from our program. When informed of this, he screamed, "What in the Hell is going on here? Nobody ever told me I couldn't take my sick daughter home from school."

I reached into our student's folder and handed him a copy of the signed contract saying, "Is that your signature?"

Although he was still angry, this took the starch out of his argument.

Seeking Middle Ground on Issues

I was often called upon to settle arguments between teachers and students. Usually students used weak defenses for their actions. Once a student burst into my office cursing. "That damn Kris! She threw me out of class and I didn't do nothing."

With difficulty, I refrained from saying, "That's probably why she threw you out." I trusted Kris but also knew that this student was usually a pretty well behaved, so I asked him to tell me what happened. After listening to his tale of woe, I asked him, "Is Kris a good teacher?"

"Yes! But that's got nothing to do with it!"

"Was she goofing off today and not trying to help you understand the lesson?

"No!"

Then I summarized our discussion. "So! Kris is a good teacher, who was working hard to teach you yada, yada, yada. Is that correct?"

"I guess!"

"And that makes her a bitch? Maybe you owe her an apology?" Take a walk and think about it. Then let me know how you plan to get back in Kris's class."

Another time, I failed to find middle ground. One of Kathleen's students refused to redo a paper after earning a failing grade on it. He was graduating that quarter and needed to pass the class. Both he and Kathleen held their ground.

Naturally he stood more to lose than Kathleen. Even when I offered to help him with the rewrite he refused. It had become a point of honor to him. Kathleen, too, believed that she would be failing in her responsibilities if she "gave him a grade he hadn't earned."

To graduate he had to complete 30 hours of composition. I suggested he might do this by registering for one of the GED classes that were held on the second floor of our building. He refused. Sadly, I was never able to find a resolution for the problem.

A year later an eighteen year old Hispanic was jailed for impregnating a fifteen year old girl. The judge involved refused to give him release time to complete his English graduation requirement so I brought his assignments to the jail. He completed them and graduated.

Black and white were not my favorite colors at alternative. I preferred shades of gray.

Building a Team Atmosphere

Among the programs housed at Lincoln was a community theater group named Merely Players, the Early Childhood program, the GED program, minority education programs and some adult intramural sports programs.

It was necessary to meet regularly with leaders of these programs to review their concerns regarding problems created by the diverse population that shared the building. Parking was a big problem. Our students arrived early and filled the parking lot which frustrated the parents involved in the early childhood program. They had to walk with their small children from distant street parking to the building. Although we discussed this often, no improvements were made until after I retired. At that time, while I served on the school board, the small green space at the west end of the parking lot was converted into parking space and parking lines were drawn. This simple change solved the problem.

Cleanliness is next to Godliness

The Lincoln custodial and maintenance staff was controversial. I received constant complaints that they did not take pride in their work. These included: "The bathrooms are filthy," "There are dust-balls all over my room." "My room is too cold." This situation brought more complaints to my desk from staff than all other complaints combined.

The custodial staff complaints about teacher's rooms were also frequent. "Her room is always messy," "Her plants shed all over the floor," or "His room is so cluttered, it's a fire hazard."

Tom, the Community Education Director, was responsible for supervising the building staff. I reported, complained and even begged for improved custodial service. Tom did not view the issue as I did.

When graffiti began appearing on the boys' bathroom wall and the custodians refused to remove it, I bought a gallon of paint to cover it and painted over it daily. Despite my best effort to catch or deter him, the vandal replicated his work as fast as I could remove it.

Finally, in desperation I called in two of our most reliable seniors, Tom and Terry, and asked for their help. My instructions included, "I don't want anyone to get hurt." I don't know what they did, but the graffiti stopped appearing.

Personal Growth

Change and growth, although rewarding, often cause discomfort. Leaving home for starting college, starting my teaching career in Stewart, moving to Lincoln, single parenting, and filling the principal's role at Alternative, although all difficult, were fulfilling.

Being a part of the task force that created the Model School was the most challenging and rewarding experience of my career. Uniting all the agencies that provided services to struggling middle level students was wonderful. Everyone from the Public Safety Director, Glen Gabriel ("I have a gun") to Nicollet County social worker, Sue Serbus ("Do you think this might work") came together to try to make this endeavor a success. Attendance at meetings was high, and complaints about shirked responsibilities were rare. Nothing was to menial or difficult. I developed a personal relationship with everyone who shared in the success of the program.

I developed a personal relationship with all who shared in the success of this program but became especially close to two Mankato officers, Marcus Erickson and Chris Boyer. They ensured the kids didn't skip school, tutored them so they could pass their classes, rewarded them with trips to Montana and Boundary Waters in Minnesota, helped them build a canoe, raised money to keep the school functioning, and built a canoe with them. They were dynamite! Today Marcus is a member of the Minnesota State Highway Patrol and Chris is the Chief of Police in North Mankato. Chris became the foster parent of one of our students. This student now works in Mankato and is a fine father of two small children.

Through my involvement in the Model School, I came to understand the details of the roles that public servants have in our lives and their commitment to our community.

My top priority when I came to alternative was to create an environment in which the divisions of the past year would end and staff members could recognize and focus on each other's strengths. Mixing work with play helped. We wrote course summaries at my lake home and and then shared a pot luck dinner and exchanged white-elephant gifts. Someone brought a mask that seemed to symbolize our need to put on a new face. Not every problem was resolved but tensions were definitely eased.

Outstanding Teachers

Carolyn Nafstead

Carolyn Nafstead was intensely devoted to the success of the students and our school. She had been a founder of the TAPP program and an original member of the Alternative staff. She arrived early and stayed late every day and was always available to any student or colleague who needed help on working through a problem. Her gracious manner and warm demeanor helped build trust with students and staff.

Although her primary responsibility was teaching parenting skills to the teen mothers, she also taught art and English. In her 50's Carolyn pursued her master's degree in counseling and ended her career as the school counselor at Alternative.

Carolyn was a leader who skillfully sought input on all the major changes at the school and who willingly compromised. She was skilled at doing this. When she shared her ideas, she recognized she was one among many.

She was invited to almost every wedding and graduation of her students and she attended all of them. Former students called and consulted her long after their graduation. She often used them to come to her classes serve as role models.

Paulette Ford

Paulette was as skilled at managing the classroom as Bill Clinton was at managing a press conference. Even the problem makers responded well to her. That is sign of a real professional.

When classroom management issues arose at the model school, I assigned Paulette to teach conflict resolution to the students there one period a day. Using the method Noel Pfifer had used in Stewart, I required the model school staff to observe and learn from her. I met with model school teachers on Friday afternoons and we reviewed Paulette's classroom management strategies and technique and they adopted strategies that fit their personalities. Both Paulette and the Model School teachers benefitted from the experience. I encountered one problem doing this. Paulette became so engaged with the model school students that she failed to arrive back to her classroom at Alternative on time.

Kris Mcguire

Kris lit up every room she walked into but she was not a pushover. She was only 5 feet tall and definitely not confrontational but she didn't back down from anyone. She had the voice of Billy Graham. Her history lectures could be heard in the balcony and if she had ever decided to have an alter call, I think the entire student body would have responded.

Her personal skills were evident not only in the classroom but also staff meetings. When disagreements arose, Kris was always able to provide calming and instructive guidance to the discussion. Her reputation for fairness and thoughtfulness fortified the positions she took during discussions of the critical issues confronting our school.

Kris was not one who got on the bandwagon or was influenced by peer pressure. She did her own thinking, but was open to changing her mind when a preponderance of evidence indicated she should.

Students learned both from her carefully prepared lessons and the manner in which she conducted herself in the classroom.

Beverly Berger

It's as simple as this. Without Beverly, the model school would have failed. Just out of college, she took the responsibility of mixing together some fairly radical and random ingredients on educating at-risk 12-16 year olds, stirred them together, and baked the bread. It didn't look or taste like any other bread but it filled the void. When the bread didn't rise very high at first, she tried other ingredients and new yeast until it satisfied all of its consumers, which was no easy task.

Beverly loved her students even when they were hard to love. She knew that if they became dropouts, they were likely destined to be failures and she took her responsibility to prevent this very personally. This motivated her to be a combination of Rosa Parks, Mother Theresa and Bonnie Parker. She had the will of Rosa, the kindness of Theresa and the go for the jugular of Bonnie. Obviously she usually got what she wanted.

The students drove her, energized her and wore her out, but they never made her give up. What we saw in her interview, is exactly what she demonstrated in her performance.

Outstanding Support Staff

Administrative Assistant
Patsy Lang

Patsy Lang was the front line infantry in every battle we fought at Alternative. When students or parents came into the office angry, Patsy was the first to meet them. When unwelcome guests, including friends of students or non-custodial parents intruded, Patsy, again, was the first to meet them. When teachers were angry, Patsy listened to their complaints. When central administrators visited, Patsy greeted them. She set the tone. She sometimes determined if the guests requests required more scrutiny before having their requests granted.

Once, a mother and father asked to see their daughter. Patsy knew neither of them, so she explained that previous approval was required for meeting with students. The man said he was just out of jail and claimed to be the student's biological father. Patsys observation and action and may have prevented a serious problem.

Patsy led the charge in planning staff parties. She was also a loyal friend. She was comfortable being a part of individual families and of the whole family of our school. Sometimes staff and kids over requested and she was clear as she explained the problem with their requests. This required confidence and strength and she had both.

Memorable Students

Emily

Emily was a 16 year-old mother when I met her at her intake. Her Aunt Kelsey, was with her. She had been a student of mine in seventh grade at Lincoln and was still warm and friendly. Emily's father, Don, had also been my student. He was quieter.

As I reviewed the handbook with Emily she seemed as ready as any 16 year-old can be to assume her responsibilities. Kelsey's presence also indicated a strong support system. So the next quarter, I was surprised to hear Emily's name come up at the Wednesday meetings where student attendance was reviewed. At the end of the quarter, she had been dropped from all of her classes and not earned a single credit.

The next quarter was more successful. Her attendance and her grades were both good. In her senior year, Carolyn suggested that Emily would be an excellent candidate for the post-secondary option. Emily agreed and began preparing for a career as a Licensed Practical Nurse. After her graduating from high school, she completed the LPN program and the Registered Nurse program at Minnesota State University Mankato.

Tom

Tom came to Alternative shortly after his parents moved to Mankato from California. His intake conference revealed that he was a chronic truant, but not a chronic troublemaker. Tom, like his parents, had a huge personality. Unlike his parents he used his in a self-defeating pattern. He was a skilled con artist.

Hoping to help him catch up as he kept falling farther behind in credits, his parents enrolled him at Alternative upon their arrival in Mankato. Here Tom used his verbal skills to assume leadership. He served on the student council, became a peer mediator, and took pride in planning activities. He also caught up on his credits and graduated with his class in 1997.

Tom served up my retirement roast at our graduation ceremony. He had the class and their guests in stitches.

Greg

Greg had quick temper and a mean punch. I met with him often and saw that he had a bit of drive and a warmer side. At one of those meetings he told me that he had completed his driver's education satisfactorily but he had not obtained his driver's license. The school district refused to release his records to the state proving this until he paid his sixty dollar fee for the course.

In an effort to improve his conduct and attendance I offered to loan him the money if he agreed to sign a contract which spelled out the requirements to obtain the loan. When I completed the contract, I asked the special education instructor to witness the signing. We all put our John Henry on the paper and I gave Greg the sixty bucks.

That was a mistake. Greg got his driver's license, bought a car, found a job and quit school.

Retirement

After completing four years of service at Alternative, I understood and appreciated the important role it had in the educational program of our district. I respected those who preceded me and appreciated their labor. They had dug the foundation, poured the concrete footings, and built the walls of the program. My role was to work with a group of decorators. We put some new paint on the walls, hung some drapes, and added air conditioning to the alternative High School.

I was part of the crew that built the Model School. We made some design errors that had to be corrected and found the original structure needed immediate remodeling. When the community of Mankato learned what we were doing, it volunteered to help us complete the structure. Service clubs asked me to tell them the story of the school and then gave contributions; retired college professors, churches, policeman and Americorps workers labored side-by-side to provide assistance and instruction; and The *Mankato Free Press* informed the public of our efforts to expand opportunities for at-risk 12-16 year-olds.

It does take a community to raise a child.

I did not retire though. My brother and partner in our used car business, Larry, died from cancer. My son, David, and I bought the business and moved it to Vernon Center. But that's another story.

WHITE BOARD ERA

District 77 School Board, Mankato, MN 1997-2002

Serving on the School Board

The final chance for training me
was on the school board.
What irony that seemed to be.
My 1st grade teacher would have roared!

On a beautiful Saturday morning in the early autumn of 1999, I read in the *Mankato Free Press* that no one had filed to run for our school board in Mankato. The district had probably 20,000 qualified candidates but not one wanted the job. The board met twice a month, and the job paid an annual salary of $2,400.00. "That should lure several candidates," I joked to Bev. "I'm unemployed. Maybe I should run." My good friend, Bill Webster, had served on the board so I had a pretty good idea of the board's total work load and had little interest in the job.

Bev encouraged me to give it a try and asked some of our friends to encourage me as well. Bill Webster called and said, "Roger, what a great idea. I'll gladly work on your campaign. When's our first meeting?" Layne Hopkins and Pat Schmidt's calls followed.

At noon on Monday I filed as a candidate. The *Free Press* article had been effective, because 13 other people had also filed.

I formed a campaign committee, raised some money and ran some advertisements. A debate was held at East High School. With fourteen candidates, I felt like an eighth-grade girl vying for the center of attention at a pajama party. Responses to policy questions were emphatic but brief and the audience learned little about how well the candidates grasped the issues.

During the debate I was seated by a candidate whose children were being home schooled. He was a very anxious man. He shifted about anxiously in his seat and was consistently critical of the public schools. I sensed from the audience responses that he would not be the people's choice.

Ultimately, Bob Sutter and I won the election with Sundstrom finishing a close third. The *Free Press* had endorsed a 29 year-old man who had been a Mankato resident for less than a year. When *Free Press* reporter, Mark Fischenich, came to our home on New Year's Day, I jokingly said, "Sure, now that I won you guys like me. Where were you when I needed you?"

Fischenich and the photographer produced a wonderful story after a fun afternoon of questioning and relating school anecdotes, theirs and mine too.

Addressing Challenges Facing the Board

The districts educational needs were challenging. The middle level program at East was housed in a shared building with the high school; the math and reading curricula needed to be updated; there were complaints from supporters of the gifted and talented and the middle-level at-risk program needed regular scrutiny. All these issues required money while public school funding was being reduced.

The Minnesota School Board Association conducted a workshop for all newly elected board members. Bob Sutter and I attended the three day workshop together and concluded from it that the board's most important job was to hire top quality superintendents and fire those who weren't. We also were instructed not to micromanage our schools. Management was the superintendent's job; policymaking was left to the board.

After serving four years on the board, I decided not to run for reelection. Privately, I was concerned about some health symptoms. I was having difficulty swallowing, my legs were growing weak and when tense, I had some mild head tremors. But, I returned to the board for another year when Noel Weber became ill with cancer. During those five years, the board focused on filling administrative roles, staff discipline, the gifted and talented program, charter schools sponsorship, transportation, building needs, negotiations, curriculum, superintendent reviews, and reform.

No Child Left Behind

The most politically charged issue was the 2001 landmark <u>No Child Left Behind</u> (NCLB) legislation that required all schools receiving funding from the 1965 Special Education Act to demonstrate adequate yearly progress for all students or to take clearly defined actions to move in that direction. Meeting basic educational standards was the talk of the country. The reform dominated local and national discussion and examination of educational practices during most of my tenure on the board.

The law spelled out the actions that must be taken by schools whose students did not make adequate yearly progress in reading and math on the standardized test given to them as follows:

1. First year – standardized tests were given to gather baseline data.

2. Second year – Schools below standard must complete and demonstrate adherence to a two year improvement plan. Students were authorized to transfer to a school which had met the standard.

3. Third Year – Schools below standard were required to provide free tutoring to students failing AYP (annual yearly progress). Students could choose to transfer to a school that had met the standard.

4. Fourth year – Boards could choose to replace staffs, establish an entire new curriculum and/or extend the school year.

5. Fifth year – The entire school could be restructured. Private educational companies could assume responsibility for educating children.

Even with the exceptions allowed for some groups of students, such as those in special education, educational leaders throughout the nation, knew, that ultimately, failure was inevitable. Once again most teachers in Mankato yawned at the law and cursed at the lawmakers, believing that this, like all the other attempts to reform education, was a fad.

Superintendents, Dakken and Waltman, however, were convinced the law was here to stay. It was a Federal mandate. The U.S. system was lagging behind Asia and Europe. Studies by educational scholars examined and compared curricula and teaching methods worldwide. When one of the educational research analysts spoke to a group of educators in Mankato his words, although we knew they were true, stung—"In America we teach too much and don't teach it well enough. Our textbooks are a mile wide and an inch deep."

The law led to some changes in our district. Dr. Dakken continued to lead curriculum studies and to make changes, but we promoted Cindy Klingl to speed the process of curriculum improvement. We also hired Gwen Walz, to coordinate the standardized testing program. She was to interpret results and assist in making necessary decisions to succeed in meeting the requirements of the law.

Gwen was a Whipple girl. Her family had been close friends of ours since we taught, socialized and coached together in Stewart. I was confident Gwen would do well. She and Cindy held special sessions for the board and administrators at which both math and reading curricula were reviewed and test scores examined. Consultants were brought in to help us.

Yet, we knew that no matter how hard we tried, we were ultimately doomed to failure to meet the demands of the law. Superintendent Waltman examined the law and located the exact position on the charts and graphs where it was impossible for a given school to achieve adequate yearly progress under the law. Although I believed the push from the federal government was in order, it seemed the law may have been designed with failure intended. If public schools failed, charter schools and private companies could govern America's educational system. The Northwest Ordinance of 1787 had set aside one section per township of the newly acquired western lands for financing public education. Now it appeared some politicians were attempting to alter the long, successful history of the federal government's role in educating the masses.

Hiring new Employees

While NCLB was the dominant single issue when I served on the board, the normal problems and issues continued to arise. Several administrators retired, resigned, were promoted, or were fired. I believed the board's most important work was hiring the best people, so I nearly always volunteered to serve on the interview committees. We hired, Mary Lou Kudela as East Junior High School principal, Shane Bair as Dakota Meadows principal, Bruce Borchert as West assistant principal and Steve Byrne as the Alternative High School principal.

Shane Bair gave the best interview I ever conducted. He was articulate, reflective, and very well prepared. When asked what role the school should have in the community, he opened his briefcase and brought out a photo album. "This is our community service class at Lake Havasu. In this photo I am helping them clean windows for senior citizens who are struggling financially. We did this on Saturdays."

Of the three candidates we interviewed, he stood out to most members of the interview team. The women on the team, however, preferred a far less experienced female candidate. Caught off guard, I had anticipated a short review of the candidates and a single vote culminating in Bair's selection. After a lengthy discussion, Personnel Director, Gordon Gibbs, suggested we might have to accept a split opinion. Under those conditions, the women agreed to accept their second choice. Bair was later promoted to lead Mankato East High School.

When the Kennedy Elementary principal position was filled, I was unable to attend the interview, which was frustrating. Bev taught at Kennedy; Tom Ommen, the retiring principal, was one of the most highly regarded elementary principals in the district; and Tim, was a local teacher who had shown himself to be very effective leader during his teaching career.

I knew none of the other candidates but with Tim's reputation, I took it for granted that he would be awarded the job. I was shocked and dismayed when I discovered he hadn't been. While Tim had earned the respect of much of the educational community, as with all in-house candidates, he may have also offended a few people. That could have played a role in his failure to be selected. I didn't read the resume of the winning candidate, Greg, nor did I listen to the interviews so my conclusions were not based on his qualifications. He later proved himself to be a very capable leader.

Improper Conduct Allegations

Although managing staff wasn't part of the board's responsibilities, sometimes—usually in high profile cases—it became part of the job. When a group of parents asked to discuss Mankato East's hockey program at a board meeting and it became clear that they wanted to fire the coach, accusing him of dangerous coaching techniques, Superintendent Ed Waltman asked for specific examples. They provided several.

They accused him of teaching techniques that endangered players. Superintendent Waltman responded, "Please give us specific examples."

"We'll need some time to verify the validity of your claims," board Chair Dan Kapsner said. "We will report back to you after we have completed our research." We asked the school board attorney, Randy Berkland, to investigate the claims. After we found the claims to be meritless, we denied the complainants the right to continue their assault.

When they were unable to remove Michaud, they transferred their kids to other schools. I don't believe their children were given much playing time where they transferred.

A cause for board intervention in management was, of course, sexual misconduct. Superintendents Dakken and Waltman preferred shared decision making with the board while addressing those delicate situations.

When I served on the board, a letter was sent to Superintendent Waltman accusing an employee of watching pornography on school time and corresponding with a male partner about sexual matters. A meeting was held with the school district's attorney to plan a course of action that would lead to a determination of the accuracy of the allegation and ensure our action was legal. We decided to examine the employee's computer. That indicating no misconduct, the case was closed.

Another time, a married secondary teacher had an affair with a married elementary teacher. Although, to our knowledge, no activity took place on the school grounds, the husband of the elementary teacher came into the school building one day screaming things like, "He screwed my wife, now I'm going to kill him." His rant was conducted as he traversed through the hallways of the building filled with children. He was removed from the building and the administration worked with the police department to assure the student's safety.

The second part of the plan required Gordon Gibbs to develop a remediation plan for the teachers involved in the romance. This included reporting back to him with plans to assure this situation or others like it, involving them, would not interfere with their professional responsibilities or our student's safety again.

Another sexual misconduct case that occurred while I was on the board, resulted in the dismissal of an employee that involved evidence of misuse of school computers and inappropriate behavior on school grounds.

The Gifted Program

Another complicated issue was the gifted and talented program. We identified gifted students using standardized tests. Parents of those denied entry routinely challenged the validity of the tests.

Our program was not a pullout but rather an enrichment program. Gifted students stayed in the classroom but were required to master a more complex curriculum and advance academically as sprinters, not marathoners like the rest of the class.

Many parents preferred the pullout model. The board was split. Board member Paul Brown spoke strongly for those who wanted the pullout because he believed gifted students were being held back under our system. His opinion seemed to be that regular classroom teachers were incapable of meeting the needs of gifted students.

I was of the philosophical view that public schools are melting pots where students of varying skills and talents learned to work together and appreciate those differences. The varied carols in Walt Whitman's *I Hear America Singing* may have been altered by advancing technology, but they still existed in all their differences. The creator of the iPod worked in the building constructed by the laborer. As youths, they shared time in a classroom. That was the glue that held our fragile democracy together.

Paul and I both volunteered to serve on the working committee that prepared the recommendations on gifted programs. After study, we met at West High School and were locked into disagreement until Curriculum Director, Cindy Amorosa, suggested, "Let's begin with increasing our advanced placement courses. I'll seek input from teachers and these new courses will open the door for the gifted and talented to be challenged but won't exclude students who don't qualify for the gifted and talented program from taking them." That was the recommendation the committee made to the full board. Paul and I both gave a little which resulted in a healthy compromise.

Transportation Issues

Transportation was an uncommon topic for board discussion, but it usually resulted in debate when it was discussed. One budget cut increased the minimal bus pick-up distance from one to one and a half miles. Another issue arose when parents who supported equipping busses with seat belts, rejected studies that indicated little was gained in the safety provided by adding them.

One rural parent called and complained that her first grader was forced to cross a road in the afternoon when getting off a bus. I brought the concern directly to Superintendent Waltman and he resolved the issue.

Behavior on buses was also troublesome. We added cameras to buses to provide evidence to parents of misbehavior and support decisions to pink slip students, denying them bus transportation. The cameras resulted in fewer behavioral problems on buses.

An annual highlight for board members were the visits to each building in the district to discuss building needs with the principals.

Roosevelt Elementary principal Joel Botten showed us a pipe that was plugged with iron and calcium deposits and then asked, "Do any of you want a drink of water?" Kennedy principal Tom Ommen offered us warm brownies in his office. When accused of bribing us he asked, "Is it working?"

There was never enough money in the budget to meet the needs of each building. Lists included lunchroom tables, desks, lockers, staircase rails and countless improvements. Principals recognized this and each narrowed the field to their most pressing needs, hoping to receive the benefit of half of that.

Reading and Math Curriculum

Curriculum changes required the most study. Any changes to reading and math could result in controversy, requiring board members to be well prepared. But research showed the United States to be falling behind in both of these so curriculum change was inevitable. That research meant little to old timers who, while discussing reading curriculum, shouted, "By God what they need is mastery of phonics. It worked for me because I took it seriously. Kids today don't pay enough attention. If they did, they'd read okay too." My early teaching taught me that phonics alone was not the answer. Research performed in the 1950's and the 1960's showed the same.

While teaching English in Stewart, Minn. students frequently complained that my assignments were too long. As a beginning teacher, I was unsure what would help them to read better, but I grew tired of hearing, "It takes too long to read all that stuff you assign." In response I tried to include speed reading in my instruction and told them, "You need to concentrate harder. Push yourself." Although tachistoscopes were being used to help teach reading by flashing words and then sentences on a screen for decreasing amounts of time, only some students were helped by them and there seemed to be little carryover from the machine to the textbook asssignments.

In 2004 the school board adopted the Harcourt Brace reading series. It used a holistic approach to the teaching of reading and followed the seven principles of effective teaching of reading. Board members attended special sessions where the research behind the series was explained and the lessons were demonstrated.

Board member, Kathy Brynaert, told the publishing representatives, "If we chose to adopt this program, we are spending a huge sum of money and demanding that our teachers put forth a great deal of time and energy in preparing to teach it. Convince us that this series will be worth it. Prove to us that our students will grow in their skills at a level commensurate with our district's investment in money and effort."

They did and we adopted the series. Cindy Amorosa reported to us that our teachers had responded to the call. She told us they spent countless hours learning to use the new series. Special education teachers, English language learner teachers and all staff who taught reading at more than one grade level prepared for all the grade levels they taught.

Since I left the board, research has continued to increase our understanding of all the learning styles of readers. Andrew Johnson, in partnership with the Capstone Literacy Center funded by the Coughlan family of Mankato, is researching a model that is designed to assist students with severe reading disabilities. It uses the latest research on neuroscience, brain imaging, miscue analysis and eye movement.

When the board adopted the new math curriculum, teachers from all grade levels volunteered to serve on a selection committee led by our curriculum director. They brought their selection to the superintendents and developed a plan for board study sessions that included University of Minnesota researchers and teachers from districts familiar with the curriculum. These presentations were not made by textbook salespeople trying to profit from their knowledge and charm.

Math was not my academic strong suit, so I was uneasy before this presentation. I feared a lengthy discussion of solving for the unknown would leave me behind in the dense forest that I had been lost in during high school algebra.

That proved not to be the case. The evening I dreaded turned out to be delightful and enjoyable. The presenter had been a high school math teacher in Moundsview before coming to the University. His comparisons of the new curriculum we were considering with the one we were currently using were sharp and crystal clear. It also turned out that he had known my high school English teacher, Leo Murphy, who had also taught in Moundsview. Murphy had been our basketball coach and was one of the more unconventional, quirky instructors I had ever known. The presenter and I laughed heartily, after the presentation, as we swapped Murphy stories.

Student Recognition

As I have reminisced about my time in high school, I have remembered how important recognition for accomplishments was to me then. I was proud that our school board honored student's achievements at every official board meeting. Superintendent Dakken read the names of each honored student and detailed his or her accomplishments.

The board also met with student representatives on a monthly basis. Board member, Ann Hendricks, arranged the meetings and set the agenda for them. Topics varied from the hot lunch program to curriculum. Ann led the meetings and encouraged openness. The students were insightful and delightful. This was the part of my board service I enjoyed most.

Budget

The most difficult challenge for the board was balancing the budget. An emergency reserve fund that equaled three months of our total expenses was required, and the remainder of our funds went to meet current expenses.

If we received a funding increase from the state, that amount was divided, as specified by law, into the correct budget categories. About 70 percent of the budget was used to pay salaries. Any remaining funds were used to improve wages and benefits for the various bargaining units. These bargaining units included administrators, teachers, custodial/maintenance, secretarial, and food service. Everyone believed there was hidden money somewhere and they wanted some of it.

Often negotiators were very aggressive in pursuing their goals. Each year that I served on the board, health insurance premium increases almost equaled the amount of money set aside for salaries. This created a catch twenty-two that unhinged board negotiators.

My situation as a negotiator was with food service. Retired teacher Marlin Spangrud, who had served as a negotiator for our teacher's union while I was on the staff, served as the negotiator for the food service staff. I considered him a friend and expected smooth sailing. No such luck.

Gordon Gibbs and I worked as a team for the board. He briefed me and shared the numbers beforehand. Marlin, knowing I was a union guy at heart, thought he saw an opening and tried to divide Gordon and me. But the total amount of money for salaries had already been set and divided among the bargaining units by the business department. The only way to get more money for food service was to take it from another bargaining unit.

Food service people were underpaid and that was considered by Gordon and me. Ed sought other non-monetary benefits that might satisfy the food service committee. He frequently said, "As you negotiate, remember your income exceeds theirs. Even though we are not in a position to offer more money, we must make every effort to increase their job satisfaction that is affordable."

At our next session Gordon opened the discussion saying, "Since pay increases are out of the question, are there some non-monetary items we might discuss that would lighten your load." Using this as a tool to satisfy food service employees we concluded negotiations.

Board members negotiating with teachers had much more difficulty. Sessions dragged into the night. Disagreements sometimes seemed trivial, and mistrust seemed to be the rule of the day. As the deadline for negotiations neared, the teachers fought for every last nickel. The money they wanted for salaries was money budgeted the last year that had gone unspent. Sometimes principals did not spend the total amount budgeted to them. These dollars were used to partially fund the reserve.

Charter Schools

Being good stewards of the public's money was always at the

forefront of our decision making. The financial impact of all of our decisions was carefully weighed. When a community group asked the board to sponsor a charter school, determining the impact of this decision required serious scrutinizing by the administration and the board.

The charter school did not fill any gaps in our district's educational programming. It seemed similar to what already existed, although its supporters argued it would be unique, based on student's interests. It could have been incorporated into the districts existing model, but a power struggle arose and trust eroded.

In order to be licensed, charter schools were required to have a sponsor. When the school board refused to serve as a sponsor it seemed to be dead. However, advocates sought other sponsors, and eventually got the Minnesota Board of Education to grant the charter.

Administrative Salaries

I was frequently accosted by former colleagues and peers who demanded, "Quit paying administrators so damn much!" But during the years I served, the board never negotiated with the superintendents. Board members completed an annual superintendent's review and discussed it with them at a day long retreat on a Saturday. When the legislature provided little new funding and the staff received little or no salary increase Superintendent Ed Waltman refused to accept a salary increase. Even when the board determined he was underpaid. This was an exceptional gesture by an exceptional man.

Summary of Board Years

My years on the board were a good experience. My colleagues were dedicated and professional and our superintendents were selfless and sought what would help students first. They held to a high standard and were detail-oriented. There were no cover-ups. Terminations of underperforming employees were rare but done when necessary and were always difficult. They sometimes had to reprimand peers who were friends. Both superintendents were firm but kind and never rigid.

They had very different personalities. Dave needed time alone after work. He worked with his hands, restoring cars, hanging sheetrock or plowing snow for neighbors. Ed was more extroverted. He knew every district employee by name and attended almost every sporting event, concert, and drama presentation in the district. He seemed to thrive on sharing the good news of our schools with civic groups.

When the East High School boys' basketball team lost to Hutchinson in the regional finals, two talented players refused to accept their runner-up awards. They threw them on the floor and walked away. Ed immediately met with the coach and players to ensure that apologies were made and that the athletes understood the concept of being gracious in defeat.

When the parents of a star football player protested his suspension and hired a well-known attorney, the board agreed to meet with the attorney to examine his evidence. I represented the board at that hearing and seeing no new evidence, I stood firm on our decision. The parents feared the violation might interfere with their son's ability to obtain a scholarship. I empathized with them but believed an important principle had been violated. By absolving their son of guilt, we would be setting a bad precedent that was unacceptable and sending the message that student violations of school rules were acceptable under the correct circumstances.

Board votes were usually unanimous. Debate preceding votes were held during study sessions. When privacy issues were involved, meetings were confidential. When division did occur, they seemed to strengthen us.

Minnesota School Board Association conferences allowed the opportunity for bonding and for learning about the issues we faced. Conversations at dinner flowed easily and we were not humorless. Noelle Weber, was a talented, savvy lady who loved a hearty laugh and didn't mind having it at her own expense. She would say, "I shop for clothes at Layne Bryant, I get more for my money there," and "Roger, I toss and turn a lot in my sleep. If I fall out of bed, I might come through the floor and wind up sleeping with you."

When Noelle was dying of cancer, Ed and I visited her. Even then she entertained us with colorful stories.

I completed my service on the board confident that our schools had been and would be good hands.

Afterword

I shudder when I think what might have happened to me had I dropped out of school. One way or another I have been a part of Minnesota's educational system from 1945 through 2004. The various roles I filled through the years have provided me with some unique insights into the changes that have taken place in that educational system and the forces that have driven them. Political beliefs, immigration patterns, technological changes, urbanization, transportation needs, child-rearing methods, labor demands and public expectations have all radically altered how schools must function to be successful. Funding to meet educations increased demands has been inadequate and unequal. Some school districts, like ours in Mankato, have fared well and generally satisfied their taxpayers.

My observations are generally limited to my experience. The vast majority of these were in Mankato where the university, the medical community and the business community are driving forces that demand good schools. Their influence is positive in many ways. They provide leadership on committees and boards. Their children help raise the bar for academic success. Their tax base provides strong local funding. Family members are part of public school staffs. With these resources cities like Mankato, St. Cloud, Rochester and Winona are positioned to become agents of change for education in Minnesota. But they, too, must undergo annual examinations to discover what ails them and how they can become even more effective.

Reviewing my experience allowed me to analyze several areas of concern in our local and state sysyems. They are:

1. **We must clearly establish improving student learning as our main focus.** The ever-increasing public demand to expand extracurricular activities comes at a price. Academics suffer! Students and parents become confused about the main role of schools. Students spend more time

developing their athletic skills than their academic skills. When I taught at West, nearly half the stuents in afternoon classes during the spring were sometimes missing. They had been pulled from the classroom to participate in baseball, softball, track and tennis. As a student, I also enjoyed these activities, but if we are to successfully reform education, we must reduce the emphasis on them and clarify that the development of students' academic skills is our primary goal.

This problem became crystal clear when the coaches of the Academic Decathlon team at West requested a minimal stipend for their work in the early 1990's. They were denied, even though they had built a national powerhouse team. This happened even as budgets for sports and other extra-curricular were increasing.

University of Maryland Baltimore County, led by Freeman Hrabowski, who was selected as one of Time magazines one-hundred most influential people in the world has no football program. Instructors there use best practices in their teaching, including cooperative learning groups. These groups allow all students to become teachers. We need to consider following the educational practices that work for them and others that are proven leaders in successfully educating their students.

2. **Political motivation cannot be the driving force behind education reform.** To their credit the authors of the No Child Left Behind law tried to raise the bar and establish consequences for not trying to meet those standards. But because of either carelessness or political motives, the bar was set too high. The law seemed to provide students with alternatives outside schools rather than improve public schools. Students who failed to meet the required standards were to be offered tutoring from

approved tutorial agencies. Licensing of these agencies was lax, and unscrupulous entrepreneurs made huge profits by using uncertified, untrained personnel. Failing students continued to fail. Our school board members, regardless of their political persuasion, wanted NCLB to succeed but knew it needed to be revised to accomplish that. Research must drive education reform.

3. **Universities must set the bar higher for entering and successfully completing educational programs.** There are verifiable best practices that teachers need to know and practice. There should be no doubt that teachers who have completed educational programs are fully qualified to fill their role in their schools. In 1962 I was not fully prepared to teach English, even though I was certified. Of the 14 student teachers I mentored, two were not ready to teach when they left. I informed them and their university professors of that. The good teachers I knew changed my life. Our students desperately need teachers like that.

4. **Educational reform must be research based.** The flexible-modular scheduling reform of the 70's seemed like it might motivate students and help them in making decisions. Teachers were trained and schools were built to implement it. But it, and other reform models like it, proved to be unsuccessful, unworkable and costly. We must be careful not to waste energy and financial resources on unproven models. I was pleased that our administration and school board recognized this while making decisions during the time I served on the board. The curriculum models our board selected were thoroughly vetted.

5. **Administrators must be more aggressive in removing the sluggards from the classroom.** All the superintendents I worked with instructed principals to deny tenure to teachers who were failing in the classroom. They were less aggressive in removing tenured teachers who were underperforming but they got better at it. The policy manual defined step by step the required procedures for performance improvement and dismissal of both administrators and teachers. While I was on the board, it was implemented with the proper regard for the privacy and the dignity of the parties involved.

6. **Students must be provided with the tools needed to find truth.** Among many surrounding distortions advertising of all sorts, particularly political ads, are filled with propaganda. If democracy is to survive, students must be skilled at discerning the distortions and lies. The 9th grade students in Mankato learn about propaganda when they study *Animal Farm*. The twisting of truth makes them angry while reading it, but I'm uncertain if there is carryover to their daily experiences with it.

7. **Unions must revise their role in public school education.** I am a strong advocate of collective bargaining. I believe management and labor must sit down together and hammer out their differences on policy and monetary issues. Traditionally, unions have been a force in improving teaching skills and sharing models of successful programs being used in school districts.

I addressed union gatherings and informed them of our model school program. Union members who attended these sessions were engaging. They wanted help in educating their at-risk middle school students. Unions need to re-engage on this issue and enlarge their role. To regain public trust they must also better publicize their efforts.

They also acknowledge the changing financial and political situation in the U.S. and show how they have improved the quality of education.

8. **Charter schools must be held more accountable.** Charter schools have been given a great deal of positive press and promoted as a possible alternative to public schools. The evidence that they do that is lacking. Recent studies conducted by the University of Minnesota show that charter school students in Minneapolis scored 7.5 lower than public schools on math tests and 4.5 percent lower in reading. Charter schools could develop an educational model that trains students to fit into the workplace. They could be wonderful research and development schools. These programs would, by necessity, have their performance measured by successfully fulfilling pre-established outcomes.

The current charter school movement reminds me of my experience with Cindy Hakes and the drama practice. Without more professional supervision this education model could burn to the ground.

9. **Read, Read and Read.** Reading assignments must again be given in every discipline at every grade level. The more we read, the more skilled we become. Students are often lazy about reading and try to use reading time in the classroom as visiting time. That can't happen. Story problems in math, learning man's structure in biology and novels in English all require reading. We must make kids read. It is the key to successful education.

10. **We must provide joy in learning.** As we become intensely focused on outcomes and measuring student achievement, we must not forget that children need to be happy every day in their classrooms. All of my favorite teachers required me to learn in their class but also made it pleasant. The best learning environments offer both learning and self-satisfaction.

11. **Federally mandated and funded early childhood programs must be available to all of our children.** I would have benefitted from early childhood. My experience in first grade may have been prevented if I had the benefit of an early childhood program. Mankato is currently reaping the rewards of increasing the enrollment and raising the expectations of its early childhood program. Research supports the positive impact of early childhood programs. This is a sound investment in the future of our nation.

12. **Extending the length of the school day will prove beneficial.** Many of our students reap the benefits of extended day school services through extra-curricular programs. Extended day services offering tutorial and enhancement programs have proven themselves. Properly done they keep children off the streets and out of trouble while they are expanding their intellectual and cultural horizons.

Final Thought

While wintering in Arizona, I am often asked what I did for a living. I always respond, "I was a teacher." I am most proud of that. I actually was given the responsibility to teach young people to interpret what they read; to organize what they wrote and to enjoy understanding the intricacies of language. From the beginning of my career I wanted to be a good teacher like Mrs. Hegdahl, Miss Riley, Mr. Mrkonioch and Mr. Avery.

Every year on the first day of school my opening line to each class was, "I have never had an alumnus of my class say to me, 'Thank you, Mr. Stoufer, for letting me goof off in your class and learn nothing.' In this class you will be required to study and learn. For that you, too, may someday, when you are more mature, say, thank you for making me learn."